I0746640

AMORPHAVILLE

edited by Bri Stokes
with works from Shonda Buchanan
and many more

HINCHAS
Press

AMORPHAVILLE

Amorphaville / edited by Bri Stokes ; with works from Shonda Buchanan.–First edition.
p.166 ; 8.5" x 5.5"

HINCHAS de Poesia Press
1. Poetry–21st Century 2. African Americans–Poetry 3. American poetry–African American authors 4. Poetry–Black authors 5. African Americans–Futurism.
ISBN: 978-1-954640-11-5
PS591.B53 T55 2025

Published by *HINCHAS de Poesia Press*
Designed by *Svitlana Matus*

Contents

Editor's Note 13

PART I:
Time

Sherese Francis 19
∆Time Reconstruction: Declarations of the Possible Multi-Verse S_lv_s Named Banna-Ka

Najah Amatullah Hylton 31
A True Education
For See-Through People

Buhlebethu Mpofu 35
The Waking: A Reckoning for the Colonisers

Lilly Lu 41
Time, a Tapestry; Me, a Weaver

PART II:
God, Ancestors & Magick

Trinity Lee 49
Crown of Thorns

Antoinëtte Van Sluytman 51
RED YOLK

Crystal Davis 57
Recipes

Cherokee Rose Collier 59
The Waiting Game

Daniel Pizarro: 61
World Bending

PART III:
Bodies

Tylyn Johnson 67
Xylophonic Notes to you
Playing Prayers to life
Black Boy, Made Warrior

Kelsey L. Smoot 73
"Parable Of The Innocent or black trans-boi roadmap"
Honest Bodies Cento

Kuahmel 77
Let's Get on a Mission

Shonda Buchanan 81
Black Woman Down

Lucy Zhang 85
The Desperate

Lysz Flo 91
wheat fields

The silence never came

When the hegemonies fall

PART IV:
Tech

Russell Nichols 103
Girls Flying High

Esteban Gaspar Silva 107
Aztlán.exe

Superintelligence Speaks in Náhuatl

The Death of Tlal[tech]uhtli

PART V:
Death

Lisa Bradley 117
Haunted

Molara Wood 121
The Stranger

Shaira Chaer 129
"Rice Water"

Nick "squidpizza" Cuevas 141
A Dog and Her Boy

H.D. Hunter 145
Natural Life

Nia Harris 149
Ease

About the editor..151

About the authors..153

HINCHAS Press
About us

Editor's Note

We've spent the past few years in a fraught relationship with Time.

The genesis of this, undoubtedly, was the COVID-19 pandemic. In the state of California, we were bound to mandatory stay-at-home orders for 10 months and six days, relegated indoors while a progressively volatile political landscape took root beyond our walls.

It's a strange experience—to be in a body during unprecedented times. I think, for so many of us, the experience can feel like straddling two realities at once. A Before and an After. The pandemic, and After. George Floyd, and After. January 6th, and After. Gaza, and After. The ICE abductions, and After.

In my own Before and After: an expansive, youthful curiosity cut short—one that I can still feel and hear and taste vividly—and an adulthood ripe with responsibilities both standard and acutely sharpened by the present: a responsibility to community, to the environment, to anticolonial thinking, and democracy—all of which are at a cosmic and cultural tipping point.

How can one avoid bartering with Time when we seem to be losing more and more of it every day?

My efforts to make sense of this have led me to lean on an understanding of Time shaped by people of color. Black folks, for instance, have always laid claim to a unique relationship to

Time. This is echoed by cultural theorist and Rutgers University Professor Dr. Brittney Cooper (whose work largely influenced the prompt our authors were asked to draw from), who argues that Time isn't neutral but racialized—shaped by white Western norms centered around commodity and control—while Black folks experience Time as nonlinear, layered with historical trauma and exclusion.

Elsewhere, Indigenous wisdom (such as that of my Hopi ancestors) says that Time is cyclical and relational, anchored in seasons and rituals that bridge the past and future.

Amorphaville is an attempt to reconcile with similar ideologies and revelations, as well as untangle our complex relationship to Time.

Our anthology is split into four sections, encompassing a wide range of genres across the speculative continuum: "Time," "God, Ancestors & Magick," "Bodies," "Tech," and "Death." Each act aims to capture visions of a world where our connections to the past, present, and future are more fluid and decolonized, aptly attuned to the simultaneous chaos and earnestness of the modern age.

In Amorphaville, these visions are woven by the voices of 23 BIPOC writers, cultural workers, and revolutionaries. Our authors were curated with intention, care, and respect to their brilliance, which is deserving of a platform now more than in any other moment in recent memory.

It is my deepest belief that artists (especially artists of color) will lead the revolution into ways of thinking and being that exist beyond the constraints of the colonial imagination. Artists are wayshowers, lighting up the pathway to a new world while simultaneously laying its foundation. We are seers, bearing the greatest dreams of our ancestors, drawing them into physical reality.

The work of our contributors achieves that very magic, and more.

As I close out this letter, I am reminded of the incredible poem "more hope" by Danez Smith, in which they affirm: "i am at peace being a grain of sand / my prayer is more sand below than above / i add my gravity to the count / i add."

May the words in this book add to our collective count towards liberation.

Bri Stokes
Editor
2025

PART I:
Time

Sherese Francis

Time Reconstruction: Declarations of the Possible Multi-Verse S_lv_s Named Banna-Ka

"I am fully sensible of the greatness of that freedom which I take with you on the present occasion; a liberty which seemed to me scarcely allowable" — Benjamin Banneker

    (M) Banna Banna Banna Ka Ka Ka

        All______Created

This dream of mine
This drum of body
These writings of time
An existence before the founding
of the United States

When in the Course of human events

        To need a proof

          Here

      This is founded in truth

    (M) Banna Banna Banna Ka Ka Ka

        All______Created

Self-educated Self-theorized Self-historicized

Self-evident

Living a life of study and curiosity
Living a life with one's own method of living
       Cultivating this space of in-between
           Near what will be structured into
           the capitol
Near what will be structured into capital capital capital

           (M) Banna Banna Banna Ka Ka Ka
               All_______Created

           Invention of a Black Horologist:

The deconstruction and reconstruction of the cl/ock
The inner workings of time resonating

The name   a token of (m)memory   a secret language
           A repetition and binding of time
           in a small pocket of space
         Bands which have connected them with
         another

           (M) Banna Banna Banna Ka Ka Ka
               All_______Created

       Laws of Nature and of Nature's God
        Timing of the S(w)__t S(p)__t

The name spoken   structures a past into a current being
The name spoken   an anatomy of time
BannaKa   holding time in the hands
             Dissecting each part
Knowing it in the hands

                                        Like a sculptor
                                Carving the wood of trees
Into the functions of time
The replications of time

(Un)alienable Rights
The rights of human nature

                                        The S(f)__t of Nature

                        (M) Banna Banna Banna Ka Ka Ka
                                All______Created
A (m)memory of (n)takoradi
A (m)memory of kujenga
A re(m)memory of com com com/put put put puta
A re(m)memory of a place built for the exchange of s_lv_s
A re(m)memory of some place to land between these flows of
being
Between these trades of deconstructions and reconstructions
Some (m)memory slips in

Amanful Ahanta
Nyame Dua
Nyumbani Mti
                                        Garab Suwo
                        Pull a piece out   Put a piece in
                        Shifting into different structures
        The calculation of each teeth   each gear   and their relations

Whenever any Form of____________ becomes destructive of
                        these ends
        It is the Right of the People to alter or to abolish it
                And to institute new____________

Laying its foundation on such principles and organizing its
powers in such form
To right themselves by abolishing the forms to which they
are accustomed
When a long train of abuses and usurpations, pursuing
invariably the same Object
Evinces a design to reduce them

> (M) Banna Banna Banna Ka Ka Ka
> All______Created

The Deconstruction of Form:
What happens to the object of time when it is lost in the mystery
of a fire?
Like a tree, it returns
To the ground
The ground roots it
Disperses it
The ground takes its elements and rearranges
Like the riffs and relations of a name

> (M) Banna Banna Banna Ka Ka Ka
> All______Created

> Senegalese?
> Wolof?
> Dogon?
> Malian?
> Ghanaian?
> Akan?
> Arabic?
> Nilo-Saharan?
> Bantu?

                                          To measure
                          An architecture of what is observed
The object becomes observer
Felt
Perceived
A meditation on the intersections of otherness
Into possession

                              (M) Banna Banna Banna Ka Ka Ka
                                    All_______Created

Re(m)membering...
Bannekke: The sweet place
Banuk Bainuk Banne: The sweetness of trunks, roots, flowers,
stems, reeds
Banakas Tanakas: What it means to belong to a place
To be positioned in time as a Sacred Sound Space as The
S(w)__t S(p)__t

                              (M) Banna Banna Banna Ka Ka Ka
                                    All_______Created

*That   train   of   absurd   and   false   ideas   and
opinions_________________________________ _______________
________your Sentiments are concurrent with mine, which are
that one universal __________given being to us all___________
made us all of one flesh_________________________the Same
    Sensations___________________ the same faculties, and
       that however variable we may be_________________
       however diversifyed _________________we are all of the
    Same ____________, and Stand in the Same relation to_____
S(f)_____T_______D*

*Δ Δ. Banna Ka's Reverberating Echo Within the Capture of
Thomas Jefferson's MyTh of Blackness (D/Ark of an Al-Manac)*

> *I make known to you___________not originally my design;*
> *but that having taken up my pen in order to direct to you*
> *________ a present___________ which I have calculated for the*
> *Succeeding__________ I was unexpectedly and unavoidably*
> *led thereto*

> *This calculation _____________________________________*
>
> *_____________________   _____________________________*
>
> *___________ the Secrets of nature, I have had to gratify my*
> *curiosity____,*
> *in which I need not to recount to you the many difficulties*
> *and disadvantages which I have had to encounter*

> (M) Banna Banna Banna Ka Ka Ka
>
> All_______Created

Transmission of Time: Many Moon Phases
Speak the motions of tidalectics:

> One cannot measure intelligence by
> the illusion of supremacy
> Of only shade and not reflection

The dynamic pull and push of a celestial object observed
Each day building into a month into a year into a century into
an age
Aged spirit in the twists and turns of the rhythms of time
Locked within the hold of this drum of time
The NK is placed —

Where one is rooted and transported   shaped into
Dis self evidence
Dis theory
Twists and turns
D/Ark

Of Al-M-NK (all my ink, my countings, my calculations)
Of Al-M-NT (my personhood, my mind, my being)
Where I find my rest in the midst of all these twists and turnings

A record response to a
calling $(K)E(L)= NTxeR^2$
An expression of the rolling around the ocean of (m)memories
How differently do I record the passing of time?
Its cycles and rhythms of nature
Its gears like an astrolabe
Like taking and binding the stars
Together in these hands
Like hearing the cicadas' cl/ick as mine

A chorus of passage through time

A call that remembers my grandfather's
and my father's passage
of an African knowing to me

My inheritance another form of time
(Un)recorded in Western science

Like Dogon in Mali
Could sense the Sirius star B without a tele______ scope
Some other sense to record the movements in space and time
Some other direction to tell their questions to

Tell the ways they have been broken open
Tell the ways they are ______________

(M) Banna Banna Banna Ka Ka Ka

All_______Created

This place to hold
My callings my truths my instructuring
My troublings my ruins my remains
My searchings

To make wood like this body cry time
By each way it is carved marked ruminated digested rewoven
Bent to the possibility of what it can become
My reflection
My mouth My mind My hands
Moving at a frequency
Like a congregation gathering — a com com com/ put put put
puta —

An o/cul/us of D/Ark

A body
Motion tracking ruins into calculations into constellations into
a fugitivity of time
Before the founding of ___________________________

The structuring of this here
Make-shifts scatterings formed into a sanctuary of observation
Into my own capitol

The measure of (K)

$E(L)=NTxeR^2 = I = NG$

The first shaping

*Δ Δ Δ. Power Radiating In All Directions (Quincunx? Or
Juroomkoñ? Or Al-M-NK)
...To extend their power and influence to the relief of every
part
Recall to your mind that time
Look back
Reflect on that time
Sense of your miraculous and providential preservation
Was a time in which you clearly saw into the injustice of a
State of Slavery
Publickly held forth this true and invaluable doctrine, which
is worthy to be recorded and
remember'd in all Succeeding ages. "We hold these truths to
be Self evident...*

Circulation of Time

              (M) Banna Banna Banna Ka Ka Ka
                    All_______Created

An endless flow back and forth
The endless intertwining and twistings of a possible
Senegalese inheritance
All flowing together
From the Cl/ick of a large MouTh

              (M) Banna Banna Banna Ka Ka Ka
                    All_______Created

The name   a symbol written from a dream
Into a journey
Into a crossing over

Where various times and s_lv_s meet and harmonize
A place to rest after a long journey

                    The name and all its possibilities:
A living spirit of time
                                        The primer of future
A positioning of the past into applications
                The return to roots and the synthesis of revelations
The drumming's transmission of power
                                The communications of reception
An unlimited broadcasting station
                                Source structuring within (s)urgency
Time and tradition built out of a siren's rhythmic flow
                        Synchronization of diasporate elements
Running at the same time into current/see
                Knockings repeatedly from the beyond of obsol_tion
Everything is current perception of prerecordings
                        The unheard's interpretations of events
The truth is a Cr/ik Cr/ak of hissstory
                                Before capitol or capital
Observations:
Can one be free outside of what is heard? "The official history?"
The date of
emancipation...the date of independence...runs on colonial
time...beyond the ticking of the colonial time cl/ock is a freedom
unheard...re/cl/aiming a time in the cl/ick of a
tongue...our dates were long before that

Be_fore Be___fore Be___fore Be____fore Be______fore
The superimposed standard rhythm of time
The superimposed standard rhythm of history
The superimposed standard rhythm of law
The superimposed standard rhythm of violence

aka The colonial metro/nome

Re(m)membering...
The name that is a measure
That is before that is beyond that is after that is between that
is change

(M) Banna Banna Banna Ka Ka Ka
All_______Created

Before bands together every Cl/ick of time
Beyond the way the standard time whips over and over
Its pestering
Its destruction
Its deformity
Its oppression
Its singular retelling of temporality
Its "official record"
Knocking constantly on the door of our temples

We the congregation declare
Our collective construction
Our own makings of

(M) Banna Banna Banna Ka Ka Ka
All_______Created

that you should at the Same time counteract_________________
_______________________________ groaning captivity and cruel
oppression, that you should at the Same time be found guilty of
that most criminal act, which you professedly detested in others,
with respect to yourselves

These standards are not responsive

To what is actually happening in time
All the measured notches
Do not reveal the entire entangled bodies of time
Our construction our deconstruction our reconstruction
What made us who we are
Do not imply there is nothing there between us
Nothing inside us
The spaces between   the scar tissue the synaptic connections

We hold these truths self-evident
We are the constant states of emergences
C(M)PT(R): A collection of multiple patterns and processes
of time to reconstruct
Building bridges across the ruptures of standard time

(M) Banna Banna Banna Ka Ka Ka
All______Created
(K)E(L)= NTxeR^2
All Time is (K)Now

Najah Amatullah Hylton

A True Education

Time when chased
like a bandit will behave like one,
when ignored like an errant child
will rebel like one,
needs attention I don't care to give
here in this world where everything is measured.

If we could measure less
and fill more,
we could attend to less
and experience more.

I just want to mosey
and piddle
and chase conversational rabbits until my voice strains.
I want to ask my students a question
with one dozen answers
and two dozen reference texts
to cite as evidence.
I want them to stretch.
They've been sitting in mental desks
for so long
their legs no longer itch to run.

The energy has progressed up to their hands,
made them hate to hold still,
kept them from the discipline
of penmanship.
While their brains
flit about like fireflies,
unwilling to pause,
to be contained,
to focus their brightness,
I want to sit with them on a beach.
Let the sun calm their pacing.
Let the heat get deep in their bones.
And make them bored and lazy.
Make them slow down long enough to see.

For See-Through People

Sometimes they say "we all we got"
like we not enough.
But a ghost of a man is your protection.
Extraterrestrial women got your back. Aliens
and angels with midnight eyes and skin are
your elevation and weapons.
They lift the load and you lift your head.
They give you space
when you're ready to flex.
They've watched you grow
and taught you to hold
your starlight between your own two hands.
Your ancestral winds blow your hero's cape.
Auntie Luck and Papa Wisdom itch your palm
and jingle in your pocket.
Uncles and elders be a circle around you as
you balance on your Mama shoulders. Beauty
and birthright move in like ocean tide, look
up at high points of golden light. Those our
eyes,
dripping in darkness,
tears match your up and down.
We got you.

Buhlebethu Mpofu

The Waking: A Reckoning for the Colonisers

I remember my grandmother's hands, calloused from generations of work that filled the Federation's coffers. She would show me the marks on her palms. "Each line here," she would say, "is a story they tried to erase." At night, our elders would gather us by the fire, where shadows danced against ancient stone walls. They taught us how our ancestors measured life not by the tick of clocks but by the rhythm of ceremonies, the cycles of harvest, and the patterns of stars. "The Dominion thinks time can be captured," my grandmother would say, her voice strong despite her years of toil. "But our time flows like water, nourishing generations."

The Dominion believed in ownership, land, labour, and life itself. They thought Time was theirs to command, parcelled into hours, and sold to the highest bidder. But Time was their invention, a lie crafted to enslave. They came with their clocks and calendars to claim all that belonged to us. Our rhythms and lives accommodate their inflexible systems, so they call us inefficient, primitive, and needing salvation. That was the first lie.

The second was the promise. "Civilisation," they called it, as they uprooted our communities, stripped our resources, and forced us into servitude. They said that this thing they called civilisation would bring progress. But the only progress they sought was expanding their wealth and power. We were to fuel their empire: reduced to numbers on a ledger. But their worst lie? Accountability. They dared hold us accountable for the destruction they wrought. When the earth beneath their monocrops went barren, they blamed us for not striving enough. When famine trailed the theft of our food by them, they called us lazy. When resistance rose against oppression, they called us savages.

In the Hollow Circle, we preserved our ways in secret. Behind closed doors, we practised our rituals, spoke our language, and passed down our stories. Each household kept a memory box—small wooden chests filled with pre-colonial artefacts, banned texts, and family histories written in our own words. These were our true wealth, our resistance against their manufactured history. They were the debtors. They extracted labour, land, and lives from us for centuries, giving nothing in return. They built their cities on our broken backs, their fortunes on our stolen land, and their futures on our erased histories.

When the Dominion's agent came to the Hollow Circle, she carried an entire ledger of numbers: hours worked, quotas missed, penalties due. She did not look at the land she condemned or the people she exploited. We were abstractions to her, debts to be collected.

"You owe the Federation twelve thousand hours," she said, her voice clipped and efficient. "You are six thousand short. Payment is due immediately."

Koro, our elder, stepped forward, his posture steady, his gaze sharp. Each dawn, I had seen him at the memorial stones, touching the names of his parents who died in the Federation's mines. His strength was driven by anger and a deep love for what had been lost. "You've come to collect what you believe is owed," he said. "Let us speak of debt, then. But not ours—yours."

As Koro spoke, the air grew thick with unspoken memories. Women who had lost children to the Federation's labour camps straightened their backs. Men forced to mine their sacred lands clenched their fists in frustration. Even the youngest among us, who had only known life under Dominion rule, felt the weight of generations rising through their feet from the earth itself.

"Your records are lies," Koro said. Where others might have shown rage, his voice carried something more potent—the quiet certainty of truth passed down through generations. Each word fell like a stone in still water, rippling through the crowd.

"Your clocks, your ledgers, your measures of worth are all instruments of theft. You speak of hours, but what of the centuries you have stolen? The labour of our hands, our children's lives, the wisdom of our ancestors? You have taken them all and called it progress."

The agent's hands trembled as she opened her ledger. I noticed a faded photograph tucked within its pages—a family portrait of her ancestors. For a moment, our eyes met, and I saw the slow, painful awakening of understanding. Her hands shook as she closed her ledger, and for a moment, I saw past her Federation uniform to the human beneath. She was young, raised on sanitised histories and taught to see numbers instead of people. "There are others," she whispered, "in the Federation. Who is beginning to question? To remember their lost histories."

That evening, as our community gathered to share meals as we always had, the atmosphere was different. Young ones sat at elders' feet, finally hearing the complete stories of their great-grandparents' resistance. Hands reached across tables, clasping in solidarity. Even our songs carried new weight—

ancient melodies that had survived generations of attempted silencing now rang with pride and purpose.

The change began slowly, like the first raindrops before a storm that cleanses. Other communities secretly sent messengers, asking how we had found the courage to stand. Our elders traveled by night, carrying our story like seeds to be planted in fertile ground. The Dominion's grip began to loosen, one finger at a time. The transformation spread beyond our lands. Their youth turned against their system, demanding answers about their family's roles in the colonisation. Some brought back stolen artefacts; others opened sealed records of atrocities. Each truth told was another brick pulled from the wall of their power.

Reckoning was not swift. The return began with the soil itself. We watched as the Dominion's people worked to restore what their machines had scarred. The earth's scent changed from metallic waste to rich loam. Native plants, once dismissed as weeds, burst through the healing ground. Their children learned alongside ours, hands in the dirt, discovering the wisdom their ancestors had tried to bury.

We documented everything—every returned artefact, every restored acre, every truth acknowledged—not for their ledgers but for our children's children so they would know how their ancestors reclaimed not just land and resources but dignity. The Dominion's people learned to work with reverence for what they had once destroyed, their hands growing calloused with honest labour rather than exploitation. For every acre the Dominion stole, restitution and restoration had been made to its rightful owners. Crops once extracted for profit now grew to nourish the community. Each seed planted was a single act of defiance against centuries of exploitation. The factories built on our labour were turned over to us, repurposed for our needs, not their empire.

"This is how healing looks," Koro said one day, watching former oppressors and oppressed planting together. "Not forgetting but growing something new from the truth."

The dawn of accountability came not with a single sunrise but with countless small awakenings. Justice bloomed slowly, like our grandmother's healing plants—persistent, undeniable, alive. When the last ledger was burned, we did not celebrate with triumph but with quiet resolution. The future we were building was not just about settling old debts and creating a world where such debts could never again accumulate. And so, the reckoning became a warning on the winds to every corner of the crumbling empire: the Time of the colonisers was over. The age of accountability had dawned.

Lilly Lu

Time, a Tapestry; Me, a Weaver

It was May again, which meant the purple flowers blooming, seasonal allergies, and exams at the Academy for Magical Weavers. Cala Lee, generally capable with two (exactly two) locks of wavy hair dangling at the sides of her face that weren't in vogue right now, but she swore would one day catch on, had prepared for all three and kept meds in her backpack for just this occasion. However, on the last item, she found herself floundering: this term's seminar final was to examine a family tree, write an autotheory on the family history, and imagine a future.

"Just say you'll be the next do-gooder," Ashlyn said, taking a bite of her apple.

Cala sighed, kicking her feet. They were waiting for the trolley together. The weekend had come, and she had two days to write this. It wasn't like her to procrastinate, but this one stumped her. "Is that what you're saying for your paper?"

"It's the easiest thing to say, and the truest, especially when you've got horrible ancestors like mine," Ashlyn said. "All the men and their unnamed wives, documented back to medieval times. I'm just going to say I want to undo all their evils."

Cala thought this was a sensible answer, but it didn't apply to her case, necessarily. Her family was diaspora on both sides, refugees and immigrants many times over. The family tree was probably fragmented, more like—bushes, or stray weeds.

And a future?

"You can just say you'll get married to the love of your life and have many kids. The professor can't contest you on that," Ashlyn said, rising as her trolley came.

Ashlyn had this breezy way of going through academic work, but as the first to attend the academy, Cala felt a pressure to do the assignment in earnest. There had been Weavers in the family before, but she was the first to formally learn how to harness the magic of archiving history and seeing into the past. Was it not some sacred duty to do right by her ancestors who hadn't had the chance?

"I'll see you this summer," she said to her classmate.

"Say hi to your grandma for me! And don't take this final too seriously!"

Waving goodbye, Cala felt a dissonance within. Yes, she *could* say she'd get married and have children—but that had never been the truth. When they'd played "house" in primary school, she never wanted to be a wife or a mother. She wanted to be in love, maybe if it happened one day by chance, but the procreative act that supposedly came later never felt *correct*.

Ashlyn liked girls and wanted to marry one, but Cala didn't know who she *liked*—if she even liked anyone that way. In her heart of hearts, she imagined cozying by a warm fire, her hand in a loved one's hand, sipping tea and composing music, maybe a cat wandering around by their feet.

And when she imagined doing more than holding hands, lips touching, and tongues dancing, her mind always shut down, the music halting. The chords didn't feel right.

She wondered if she was wrong, if she was a dissonant chord in the family tree that wasn't right, a weed herself.

*

Her grandma made her duck and ginger soup that night, having sensed her inner turmoil. When they sat down, she poured her troubles out.

"It's silly, I can make something up," she said, shaking her head in embarrassment. Her Popo had better things to worry about than a school assignment.

But Popo only rose, her pink fuzzy socks scuffing the old tiles, went to the basement, and emerged a minute later with a scroll.

"What is that?" Cala asked, marveling at the rough edges.

"This," Popo said, adjusting her round red glasses, "is our family."

"We—have a family tree? An actual documented record?"

"Something like it."

She unraveled it, and it rolled out as if sighing at her touch. There was Weaver magic here. The scroll stretched three feet and had perfect, fine calligraphy scrawled across it.

What lay before Cala wasn't a family tree but an abundant, sprawling family garden. Names written in configurations that appeared more like constellations than straight lines. Most remarkably, names of all genders, not just men and their wives, and not just the people who went on to have children.

And as Popo hovered her fingers over names that seemed to float like stars among the flowers, with no line connecting them, the future seemed also to spill out before Cala like the richest tea staining parchment gold. As her grandma spoke, she conjured a folk Weaver magic, visions of the women rising in front of their eyes from the parchment as if they were in the room with them.

Lee Suyong. A woman six generations before. She was a Weaver like Popo, able to conjure magic through her art. Her art? Embroidery and fashion. She never married, but it was said that she lived in a beautiful home with her long-time childhood friend, and they cared for each other all their lives.

Lee Rentang. Another woman, Popo's aunt, who never married and never showed any interest in getting married. She was a singer and a theater actress, scandalous for the times, but she was in several newspapers, known for her beauty and talents. She was never lonely. She grew old and remained fabulous.

Lee Yuyu. A woman ten generations ago. A renowned poet in her village who kept many birds. She was proposed to five times in her life, and turned down each one. She ended up living with her aunt, who also enjoyed a life of singledom.

"And," Popo said, her finger hovering over her own name, "Lee Tsang. I married your grandfather out of necessity and companionship, but if I lived in a time less desperate, I probably would have stayed single, too. I enjoyed the idea of dating, but not much else."

"You too?"

Popo nodded, no hint of shame or regret in her eyes.

"But what if—what if I'm a weed?"

"Weeds are very beautiful, and they visit your grandma's garden often, so I don't mind." Popo clicked her tongue. "Plus, if you turn out to be a Weaver of gardening, then you can make anything beautiful."

Cala laughed, because she had no green thumb. She suspected her Weaving magic was in music composition anyway, the way that the erhu sang at her touch, the way that ancient flutes were easy for her to pick up and intuit without much training.

"All of these people had meaningful lives, regardless of what they did, or how many children they birthed. That is not who you are. *You* are who you are."

Cala soaked in the words that hovered around her like a happy mist, and then she marveled once more at the document. "I've never seen something like this. How did you find it?"

"I did my own research," Popo said, "wove together stories my own grandmother had told me. I wanted to include ngo ge gating, including leiyun." *My family*. Including the women.

All of these women, all asexual, like Cala.

Asexual. She'd never allowed herself to think that word before, even in the privacy of her own brain.

But it ran in the family, apparently. She wasn't alone. And they had lived full, joyous lives.

Popo smiled at her, her eyes crinkling beneath her scarlet glasses. People in town loved Popo for her eccentric sense of fashion, her bold patterns.

She touched her own hair dangle and smiled back. Weaver magic was important, because history was important. And if the past was healed and reckoned with, the future had more of a chance.

And the future was winking at her with possibility—possibilities rolling out before her like fields of flowers, in all directions, just as they had, she imagined, before, and just as they would again.

PART II:

God, Ancestors & Magick

Trinity Lee

Crown of Thorns

the sea you must wade
the deep you must touch
the waters we were born in, dark and unfamiliar
the horror of blue emerald, tethers to the edge
free yourself from the top of your head
let the rock of the waves toss it loose
the bristle and wool
the freedom where the conch crawl is open to you
the surface erupts, and what emerges, a heart
an arm, a leg
a truth, a peace
a crown of thorns,
red washed away

Antoinëtte Van Sluytman

RED YOLK

It's moments like this that define you. When the necklace of minced pork summons the wok to life with the sizzling wail of hot blistering oil, its aromatic redolence of red pepper invading the senses, and your soul sings.

It is with such insipid simplicity—fragrant dash of native cultivar pinched between your fingers, the twist of tender red meat into links in your hands, the sulfurous haze of sweet spices permeating the air—that you navigate the cusp of ecstasy. You taste achiote on your fingers. Motion the wok that has been passed down to you from ancestor to ancestor. Move through the temperature like a dancer crossing the room. Encore.

This song, this great declaration of smoke-kissed meat, dazzled in the complex flavor of your heritage, is your great symphony. You are its composer.

Smell that? It makes you smile, doesn't it?

This little power you herald over the cruel, war-torn world around you is power nonetheless. You were the scion of scent in this small world of hungry patrons seeking refuge from the world. But the greatest prize salvaged beneath the heart of your small thatched roof was undoubtedly the chorizo. The House of Chorizo never emerged in the same place twice. Loyal patrons knew how to navigate the barricaded alleys, read the language traced in mounds of cumin in the spice markets, and exchange information beside bone white churches they were forced to construct for a God they did not recognize. The people of these lands always found a way to your doors. To the mountains. You reach for the trio of eggs balanced neatly beside your wooden spoon, and maybe your trance of raw egg and meat is enough to deter your mind from the abysmal nature of what awaits beyond this small paradise.

Smell that? Almost ready.

Crack. You cleave an entrance across the white shell, wide enough for tears of gold paradise to seep in between. In goes the first egg.

Across the room, you see the faces. They appear honed by experience, but you know they are beyond their years. Conscripts back from battle. Here to be saved by the batter of egg and red pork. Focus. Don't burn the eggs.

The precious sphere hits the rusted edge of the wok, spilling its golden innards into the embrace of sizzling chorizo.

These moments define you, remember? Pay attention.

It was intimacy from a distance, for you don't even know any of their names. You know them only for their orders and the moments they offered you. A transaction as fragile as that smooth white eggshell you bludgeoned open with a simple tap. That's all it takes to upend an entire person's world. To cleave open an abyss where peace and unity once reigned. A tap. Crack.

A pinch of garlic now. Pick up the knife.

Time to pat the maize into shape. Pat, pat.

There. Sitting in the corner beside the hearth would've been one of your regulars. A native with kind eyes and a braid that reached the floor. Their order: Gallo pinto and a tamale with a side of chifrijo. Their first bite was like witnessing a lost child returning home, clinging to the grip of their mother as if afraid to ever let go again.

The last time you saw them, you noticed their braid had been cut. Shaved down to that of one without identity and branded against the temple by an empire. They cleaned their dish of rice, politely tipped their head before slipping out into the night. That would be the last time you'd see them again. Pat, pat.

Then the one who claimed the shadows nearest to the door. A spiritual leader who spoke to spirits. Her hands were unquestionable, which you found to be the most distinguishable. The men came for her the next day when she burned their monastery.

Her order: Aroz con pollo, plantains, and café con leche.

You've stopped smiling now. Your mind wanders too far.

Pat, pat.

There was a warrior with a great big laugh. He sang mighty songs that mothers passed down to their sons. You can no longer remember them, can you? The day he stopped singing was the first time you burnt the eggs. He only ever ordered the chorizo con huevo.

Go on. Slide the onions in.

The chair beside the hearth, the shadowy corner near the doorway, and the small terrace remain empty. You know instantly that the woman whose loud entrance broke your trance earlier was related to the man with the great laugh. The woman finishes her meal, approaches, reaches out, and offers you more money than you've ever laid eyes on before.

"It was my son's savings," the woman says.

You refuse the money because you are more accustomed to giving more than you take. When she insists, you question her reasoning.

"This is ours. It shall remain so." She gestures to the space around us. "This place must remain here well beyond our time. My descendants will taste your food, and they will think of great Awapa and strong mountains. They will come home."

You accept the money and will never see the woman again. You will hold onto your mother tongue, harbored between your lips like precious spice, until the day her descendants meet you. Nobody ever questions your age or that you might be older than that elder woman who left you a great fortune. Age will never claim you. You've been immortalized by the heart of your people. You are a secret of the mountains, a legacy of howling steam and hissing butter, and your wok will speak of great Awapa and strong mountains, until those seats fill again.

It is for these moments that you live, that define you. Do try to remember.

Smell that? Eggs are ready.

MILK HONEY & SOUL

Here I rest.
Head-dizzy,
I cast a spell on you,
A summer breeze blows sweet through cities,
Glistening sweat and laughter tainted with magic,
Milk like holy water,
So contagious,
Here magic exists.
Here children paint the colors of Africa on trains,
Here they paint portraits of heaven on corpse buildings,
With dark chemicals.
Here music is a Goddess sprung from the soil,
Concrete crack from joyful noises and shoeless dancers,
Here neglected artifacts are turned gold when dipped into the
honey mouths of school girls,

Here everyone wears black crowns,
Glistening with soul,

Justice is united in secret meetings,
Held to each breast,
Here Angels sleep in project buildings,
Where there is only struggle, justice, and love.

Eyes bloodshot,
But she knows her children will carry a jar of honey and soul in
their front pockets,

Here is where God smiles upon,
Watching sightless magic men play her music on piano keys,
Who begin movements printed in blood, sweat, and tears,

As the children paint burning buildings gold,

Melanin loved by the sun,
Children run and play in the holy water, Of fire hydrants.
Here magic exists.
Here is soul.
Born from nothing.
And it ignites from oppression,
And them rich men.
Will never understand.
That Angels rest here.

Crystal Davis

Recipes

I am a kitchen witch,
I dazzle my pots and pans with sparks and flames,
Chop my vegetables with precision.
With the help of spices and seasonings in my cupboard,
I can travel to a hundred countries and never leave the comfort
of my kitchen.

My flavors range from the
savor of Creole epis,
Thai coconut curries,
Indian paneer and butter chicken,
Chinese pastries,
Soul food with black eyed peas,
mac and cheese, and candied yams,
sofrito en arroz y habichuelas con pollo.

I've got these recipes cooking in my soul,
Sweet potato conjure will have you sweet on me.
Kissing my every footstep after you devour my sugary sweets.

A pinch of cayenne pepper will have you meowing at my feet, in
a blaze of passion over these smoked neck bones and collards.

The witch in me will toss a pinch of salt over my left shoulder.

I'll knock on the wood of my countertop
just to keep the bad juju away a bit longer.

Recipes come to me like experiments
in the science lab, seasoning, and tasting to get the flavors right.

Chef's kiss when my taste buds scream in delight.

Cherokee Rose Collier

The Waiting Game

I ate it all,
Licking up and crunching on....
The world.
Microscope eyes awaiting their latest discoveries.
Bugs swarm between my toes reminding me I have feet to stand
on.
To walk, to run
Twenty-five means nothing with feet like these.
These feet I share with five-year-old me.
I bury myself
Sand, water, soil
Bury me with the Earth Mother and call her God.
At least the coffin is made out of wood.
Let her envelop me
Let me conceal myself in her
Licking a shell to make it shine,
Eating sand to scrape clean what's inside.
Refusing to protect my eyes from the sun.
Let it burn.
Let my retinas retain the life I once had
Let them burn with blissfulness of the past
Let me be who others read about.
While they flit from page to page,

I flit from sky to moon, awaiting the daylight.
Then do it all over again.

Daniel Pizarro:

World Bending

Immense gratitude for Octavia Butler

If God is change
Then I am an embodied spirit,
That is ceaseless,
Endless,
And expansive.

An embodied spirit
Trapped in flesh
That outgrows itself every seven years or so.
Mesmerizing to think
That on a microscopic level
This flesh internalizes God
This flesh practices the word of God
If God is change,
Then my transness is nothing short Of
divine orchestration.
I am my creator.

Molded by the current of time
Eroding the segmented burdens
Experienced through existence.
Funny how moments in time

Burden and imprint into our psyche.
Solid like boulders piercing
The flow of a river.
Time erodes all boulders.
If God is change,
Time is the vacuum
Through which we feel God.
An endless force.

To accept God as change
Is to accept God without
Casting moral judgments on what is.
Good and bad serve no purpose
Other than to aggrandize the ego of the sinner.
Survival is outside the confines of morality.
Death is a ritual,
But we are not each other's executioner.

I see you in your vastness.

A sweet divinity emerging
As life lapses through cycles
Unraveling the being you were always meant to be.
Your reaction towards change
Towards God
Is the language of creation.
Your body and the actions you make with your body is a
conveyance of your divinity.
Our choices express our divinity
An endless set of possibilities
That changes with every fleeting thought, emerging feeling, and
Conscious or unconscious action.
All that we touch changes
Your intention is magic

Your actions are sacred
If God is change
Then the power to create new worlds is at our fingertips.
So I ask you beloved,
What can we create?

PART III:

Bodies

Tylyn Johnson

Xylophonic Notes to you

With each stroke of the keys comes a matching strike of
another key, glazed marble to glassy wood.
Two-toned with ivory and patterned with sable,
and stained with a kaleidoscopic array of melodic
wedges,
Creating a painting to never be forgotten,
And so the man jumped into it and swam in the acrylic teal,
the scent reminiscent of his nails freshly painted
with the crimson of the phoenix.
I knew him once upon a time,
his complexion the perfect shade of darkness,
just dark enough to turn him into coal under those
surgical lights,
waiting to be pressurized into the sparkling beauty of a
flawless diamond.
Well,
diamond-in-the-rough.
for he had been called to cast his ebonic hue
in the name of a space colored pale by the harsh winter.
Til he took the plunge into the bleached waters and realized
the potion was no milk or honey, but poison
and murderous.

As the seaweeds took hold of him, he
thrusted skyward once more,
and so he dragged out a root, gasping for air
        the breath in his chest returned with sharp vigor,
        stabbing him for his desperate abandonment of color
    to obtain a power not meant for him to be given.
No.
        He hath another power deep within, to be
        drawn out
                through the stories he was birthed from,
                through the lives he changes with mere
                words,
                through the embrace of the reflection he
                faces in the mirror,
and thankfully,
        I was able to wash the world anew with the bewitching
tincture of rapture

Playing Prayers to life

With the flick of my thumb,
I move a digitally-rendered being
to craft a story of my own within
the well-defined world
that I witness upon my screen.

The books I read in my youth,
> now given to a visual form of storytelling wherein I
> become
> an active agent in the storylines I've tied myself up in.

Press a button and I traverse a world
imagined in the language of numbers and code,
> painted by their thoughts come to life

Of course, this act of movement
through my own avatar, myself given divine will or status
all comes after I've built this incarnation of mine
from the options of afro and bald and cornrows
with the touch of deepened voice and glasses,
in the loose-fitting wear of a sultry masculinity, kissed by the
flow of femininity
despite how, even as a Creator, I am made to assign my own
gender,
a thing far from being reckoned with in this reality
as I seduce myself with the play of androgyny.
Still, in all my divine knowing, I assign traits to this
messiah and messenger that I send into the new world I've
entered,

but I control the lines that move them in their fate.

And so long as my memory remains well, uncorrupted,
I decide the fate of this scripted world
at the tips of my fingers,
though, sometimes,
my hands cramp
from the pressures of controlling so many, so few, possibilities,

and trying to replay this story
in all the ways I can to reimagine how it ends,
            knowing the only way it ends
            is by way of me losing my power

And I am stuck contemplating
whether I ought to reclaim it,
            or to simply allow this story to be shelved in some distant
and forgotten library.

Black Boy, Made Warrior

I was the kind of Black boy who dreamed themself a warrior. Trained by an older brother through the sacred tales of *Naruto* and given a taste of a warrior's power once controllers were placed in our hands. In the mythologies and histories of Japan, I crafted myself a wielder of blade and magic and melanin, speed and strength far beyond what might become real in a scrawny body that knew more of books than bulk. But in my studies of these hallowed stories, grounded and mindly, I discovered a figure that deserves his praise, a real-life model of all that we thought impossible.

His name: Yasuke.

He was *the* African samurai before Samuel L. Jackson brought his voice to an Afro-headed, and named, muthafucka. Yasuke was THAT nigga.

To become mystery and legend in a land that knew nothing of his roots, to traverse the castes of samurai of Japan and slave to European colonizer. He was the kind of warrior I thought I could try to be. In Him, a man whose story is more untold than deserved, I found a power and a muse.

With origins expectedly ambiguous from the erasive nature of a young colonialism's slavery, this man was birthed from one of the thousand tribes of Africa. Not so unlike the little Black boy who comes from a lineage with a story scarred by the chains of slave trade on the opposite side of the world. And somewhere along the way, he found himself under an Italian missionary in Japan, whether as slave or hired bodyguard, his name now finally recorded in Japan. In war-torn country, he became a conversation partner of a Fool-turned-Demon King, a

Unifier who might have offered him the name we know him by now, a possible fusion of the African warrior's heritage and his new place beneath falling cherry blossoms. It was in Yasuke that I learned a land far off from my feet's knowing.

A man whose dark skin had been scrubbed cause they thought him made of ink and earth. They ain't know of the peoples who bore dark skin that had tasted many years and climates of sun. They never knew of hair that could be loc'd like gold, fros fixed with cherry blossoms, braided in rows and rivers. In He whose fate remains largely unknown to us, historical imagination fused with a child's ideation for warriors and honor, all in me. And in historical precedence, he was named beast in the last moments of his recorded story, the last defender of the adult child of a man labeled a demonic thing. How Black boys are made to grow up quick, to engage in wars they should have never known, home life, street life, nationwide. Far from the only one, hell, possibly the least-damned Black body there.

There h/we was, moving between languages, battles fought with a grace not believed possible in t/his being. And the scary thing for me, Black boy leaning into all he could be, the last thing we heard of Yasuke was that his living body was returned to the West, or had otherwise disappeared

somewhere in this land of grand, paper castles and golden temples. How our warriors always end up returned to their oppressors, or stranded with no one left to fight for. Isn't that a hell of a thing to know now? When the Black boy I used to be would have painted Yasuke just as alive as the spirits placed in a katana, warmth found in cold bodies, meaning derived from bloodied things.

Kelsey L. Smoot

"Parable Of The Innocent

or black trans-boi roadmap"

It's November, and babies are vanishing from the planet quicker than

[we]
would ever accept if they were anglo. And instead of organizing, or using our fists we
[must]
vote, according to the *"in this house we believe"* front yard sign liberals. The ones who
[swim]
 in resort pools every summer, which have never cradled a Black body, but would swear
[through]
stark white veneers that they have Black friends and Brown ones and Yellow too and want
[the]
the world to be a safer place for this magnificent friend rainbow. Spewing white-hot
[swill]
like the promises made on a campaign trail. Leaving empty brown arms from Uvalde

[to]

Rafah—arms which now encircle only themselves until sleep comes. If this poem could

[reach]

anyone, I would want it to be a child who has not yet known suffering, a being barely beyond

[a]

twinkle in their father's eye. Unmarked by the pink and blue binary or the red maga cap and

[pink]

pussy hat divide, or the billionaire versus the not-enough-food-to-feed-a-human-whose

-[nipple]-

needs-to-feed-another-human crisis. Yes, I hope this finds you still yet perfect, living in

[paradise]

Honest Bodies Cento

I conceive of my life
as a journey toward something:
anomalous intimacies,
the idioms of chemistry,
attempts to recover
what has been forgotten

We need to face the terrifying,
simple act of claiming pleasure;
that shattering or implosion of self,
the deviancy assigned to evolution

Imagine our predicament
if we coexisted,
intertwined with new high-pink flesh,
buoyantly dressed,
before the summer solstice

Sweat bees and mud daubers,
call them freedom fighters,
—brow puckered and sucking teeth—
find fault, cling,
reject the path we have cleared,
its angular turns ruptured
in Washington's sweltering heat

And still,
I view them with hope
and not despair
Everybody knows somebody

readying up for honesty,
and moments of transcendence
They have simply been taught
not to speak the truth of their bodies

Kuahmel

Let's Get on a Mission

We've established the problem
We've worked the problem
The problem is deep-seated in Black minds
to the point the problem is
we have all bought in that we are doomed

But are we?

Maybe we have sat with doom too long
Deep seated in situationship

Reject that doom from your room...now!
Because the time is now
Time to move on this moment and TAKE OVER!
Move on this world and TAKE OVER!
Secure this new future in our hands

We get on a mission
To the next level of power
The next level ethic
Political ethic,
Education ethic,
economic and financial ethic

All existing platforms we make part of our credit

See our annual voter ballot and raise it
Staying daily in the face of elected officials
If they cannot get it done,
The office is ours for which to run
If existing businesses ain't got what's needed,
we start one up, two up,
whatever to meet it

We reclaim the local school districts
Make them teach beyond the test and the
textbook
Rupture the school-to-prison pipeline
Flash flood the colleges!
Dominate business, science, tech, engineering,
math, law, medicine
HBCU to UCLA,
Wherever we wanna learn shall be a divine
mind residence!

If your voice has ears,
drop game on those who need what you know

Conscious people, plant them seeds
You may not convert someone overnight if at all
That doesn't mean your knowledge
Ain't the vitamin supplements our people need
Churches, you have an army organized
in barracks with crosses attached
Show them what Jesus could REALLY do
See your prosperity gospel and raise it with
liberation theology

Gangsters, thugs, D-boys,
we embrace your rider spirit
Ride with your people, for your people
Be real Black for us and for you
And to all who've been locked up or on the P,
lobby hard to get your rights back
So sooner, not later, you get right back in the
lobby of living!

Let's get on this mission
gather this collective into closed ranks
elevate value of Black life
destroy double standards in society
make Black section of town the place to be
Everything we need within walking distance
Every hole plugged, every street clean
No disrespect from vandal or gentrifier
Black arts making events that are the ultimate
attraction
the house that we built to our satisfaction!

I can and WILL say more, but now
you're within mindshot of these words
you're inspired to add to our reality
Band as brothers and sisters as we dance
Let us ride side by side
Let us unite and conquer
Let us show and prove our power
Let us get on a mission!

Shonda Buchanan

Black Woman Down

*(A Living Poem for Breonna Taylor, Nia Wilson,
Latasha Harlins, Eula Mae Love, Sandra Bland,
Ketanji Brown Jackson, Fani Willis and all my
sisters who have crossed over unnecessarily,
those still fighting, and for my mother.)*

The breath.
Sycamore spores
and black girlhood calcified
in a copper memory.
Inhale.
Touch the bruise until it fades
into a place that can never be seen again.
Mama.

Pour all your blood
into a thimble and top it off
with "why daddy always beating me?"
And when she grew up,
"shake that moneymaker."
So she did.

The breath is a swollen kiss
in the eye of a tornado. Black woman.
The breath is a copperhead snake under your stairs.
Black girl.
The breath is 13 children that pushed themselves
out of her body like beautiful bloody fists.
But the black girl-child, sister, aunt, cousin, grandmother
is still breathing.

This breath, in each instance
it is the thing that we need the most,
the thing we take for granted,
and the thing that will kill us all.

The Middle Passage breath.
The concubine breath.
The they-killed-my-son-my-daughter-for-no-reason breath.

And I am returned:
I am writing with my eyes closed in the slave ship.
In the hull. Portuguese slaver on top of me.
I am releasing my spirit.
I am out of body to survive this.
I am writing on the saltwater
writing to the shark gazing at us to save me.
I am writing with my eyes closed.
Seeing the granddaughter born
of his blood but not his name. Not his country.
Under him, I am breathing, unpeeled, a historical footnote.
A lost moccasin. Broken teeth rattling in me.
The breath is my childhood running
in a grassy meadow, then dancing on pimento seeds.

But I will not die here.

The breath is a circle of black women
strung like garlands around your neck.
The breath a sweat lodge in heaven.
The breath a doppelgänger. Asking,
is that my breath or the breath that breathes like me?

The breath is wagon trail quiet.
Slaves crawling against the Choctaw night.
Ant beds and river beetles in my hair.
Holding my urine so the dogs won't smell me.

The breath is a beast.
Ravaging through the body caverns
like dragonflies in love.
In the first marriage, the first molestation,
the first bruised lip; it won't let you die.

Your heart pumping viciously
anyway with the love for that man who said,
"if you leave me,
I will kill myself."

The breath is sugar water rolling
through a black woman's body until we sleep.
The breath is your black child asking you
to keep your black power opinions
and poems to yourself.
The breath is a river crashing into the mountainside
until there is a hole large enough for history to come through.
The breath is Latasha Harlins reaching for orange juice.
The breath is Sandra Bland's rope silently singing.

The breath is Eula Mae Love dropping the knife and turning.
The breath is Breeona Taylor sleeping in her bed.
The breath is eight bullets: 1, 2, 3, 4, 5, 6, 7, 8, silver kisses
ending her dreaming.
The breath is a tree wishing away the noose,
the chainsaw, the white gaze.
The breath is Ketanji Brown Jackson
answering senators' ante-bellum laced questions.
But she will not die there.

The breath is a black woman down.
Is all my sisters who have crossed over unnecessarily
but I, we, will not die here.

Exhale.
However many generations it takes,
you still fold into the pain of loving,
men, families,
societies again and again,
children
the surviving them, the birthing them,
the giving them away,
the dying, the coming back to life.
The breathing. The breath.
Black woman.
The door is always open.

But I, we, you will not die here.

Lucy Zhang

The Desperate

The women in my family give birth to children without men. We came from embryos developed from unfertilized eggs pried from our mother's stomachs and locked away in safes where we were left to grow. We birth children easily and painlessly if the embryo is extracted early, while it's small enough to slip through an incision the size of a fish bone. My sisters prefer to nourish embryos in their bodies longer. They believe it will increase the child's chances of survival. Unfounded science. This is a numbers game, and the more embryos you can extract and lock away, the better your odds.

I have created hundreds of embryos. None survived. My mother had me on her third attempt, and my grandmother had my mother on her first. I seem to have lost the trait. But fertilized eggs are cheap, and the incisions don't scare me. The bothersome parts are cleaning out the safes and finding rotten, wrinkled masses of embryos. I throw the dead babies into the compost. The fruit trees love them, and the pears and apricots grow larger and sweeter when nourished from remains.

"Think about growing them in your body a bit longer," my mother tells me. "Extended nourishment will increase the likelihood of survival."

I survive on fruit trees extending from the backyard into the forest. Our bodies react poorly to meat. Meat stops our eggs from developing and turns our hair brittle and bones soft until all that's left is rice-paper skeletons. All of my ancestors were raised on the same fruit trees, and our source of nourishment hasn't changed for generations. I'm not sure how leaving an embryo to fester in my body will make a difference.

"That's not necessary," I tell my mother. "Just because it took you almost no tries to get results doesn't mean everyone is the same."

A week later, I find my mother digging through the safes in my room, retrieving the embryos produced in last week's round of trials. Each safe is splayed open, covering most walkable surface areas. She plucks out the dead embryos like weeds and presses them into a plastic bag, each dried mass crunching into the other as she compresses the plastic so she can fit more.

"So much wasted space," she murmurs. "You need to clean up earlier. Only if you're proactive can you start your next round and stop dwelling on these failures."

"I'm not dwelling on anything," I reply. I keep the embryos in the safes longer than necessary because I want to give each batch a fair, fighting chance: as long as one might be alive, the others deserve a chance to claw themselves back to life.

"You need to take this seriously," my mother says. "If you don't successfully create an embryo that can survive past its time in the safe, you could die."

We die if we haven't birthed a viable child after a certain amount of time. A part of our body shuts down, and even the most nourished and fertilized of fruit trees can't resurrect us from this state of dormancy. We saw this happen to my cousin, who had always been wired a bit differently—uninterested in harvesting the fresh plums and peaches threatening to split open in the summer, indifferent to the accumulating number of eggs growing in her stomach and the embryos fighting to break free. My cousin refused to undergo a single incision to release an embryo before she died. We never learned why. I suspect she wanted to have a child the "normal" way: with a man, after lovemaking, accompanied by the pains and swelling of her stomach. *Silly girl*, my grandmother would say. *Chasing a fantasy.*

I always covered for my cousin and watched over her apartment when she disappeared for days to meet men in bars. I had no idea where she found these social gatherings, especially since most of us actively avoided men whom we saw as threats to our survival. But she'd occasionally return drunk to her apartment, a man propping her up, one arm wrapped around her shoulders, and they'd disappear into her bedroom for the night. "They stay for too long," she often complained to me. "I expect them out before I wake up the next morning. Breakfast isn't free, you know." Not that these sessions of intercourse produced viable embryos.

"How do you identify the strongest if none of them are strong?" I ask my mother.

"Strongest is relative among the group. You only need to wait for all but one to die."

I frown. My embryos keep dying like flies drawn to a furnace, a cycle of spawning and shriveling. Their deaths no longer upset me. It takes too much energy to grow attached to every single egg, and even more energy to memorialize the emotional departure once they die. Any spare energy is best spent improving my odds of survival: re-organizing the bedroom to optimize for sunlight that might encourage stronger growth, more drastic pruning of the orchard to yield more nutritious fruits, singing for hours in front of the safes to coax the embryos into lasting these days in the dark.

"There is weakness in your blood," my mother tsks. "How you were the one to survive, nobody knows. Honestly, it was very close between you and one other. But the other one was too quiet. We thought it was dead, and by the time we'd retrieved you, the decision had already been made."

Once a decision is made, all remaining embryos must be burned. This usually isn't a problem since they're already dead, but even if you mistake one for dead, it must be burned.

"You'll die, you'll die any day now," my mother laments. "And if you die, I'll need to have another child."

Daughters stabilize their mothers' old bodies, like stakes wedged so deep in the ground that they've become part of the earth. I suspect it works as some kind of genetic echolocation: an evolutionary need to persist, confirmed by a daughter's existence. The women from my family die quickly without that tethering, as trees would when uprooted, roots left to dry. Before my cousin died, her body had already shrunk to one-third of its original size, her head disproportionately large compared to her limbs, and her fingers curled inward and stiff. That's how the weak die. We are not supposed to interfere.

My mother and I live separately, but close enough that she can walk over and not struggle to carry a tray of strawberry Napoleon cakes. She rolls the pastry out with her arthritis-plagued hands, resulting in dough too thick and uneven to stack to the heights of eight or twelve layers. She still makes enough pastry for eight layers and saves the leftovers in her pantry as snacks to eat plain. She claims she dislikes fanciness even though her existence seems to revolve around beautiful desserts, intricately floral clothing, and trips to islands planned down to the minute. She visits weekly to check up on my embryos, scrutinize the survivors (of which there are none), and lecture me about how she's withering away with each week of failure. She does this while stretching her shoulders and back with the resistance bands—a purchase I made thinking deeper stretches might shake free stronger eggs—and contorting her arms into odd angles while letting out small sighs and grunts of relief.

I've begun to pretend I am not home, though. I barricade my windows with boards and sit in my room, quiet until I hear her turn away from the door and leave. Eliminating her presence should at least reduce the stress on the embryos in my system. I hug my arms around my torso, as though the warmth can circulate into hundreds of tiny lives long after they've left my body. I drag a scalpel a millimeter across my skin, below my navel. I cup my hands below the cut to catch blood from spilling and retrieve the next batch. Then I crawl to the small, jewelry box-sized safes where I deposit the fresh embryos. I've learned to be efficient.

Lysz Flo

wheat fields

After the smoke clears—& liberation has cost us too much
we gather the seeds they wanted to extinguish out of us
& begin to rebuild

they tried to disintegrate our dreams
uproot us from our motherlands
on occasion they succeeded
but even when the moon is eclipsed it shows itself again & so
we rise

returning to wombs of lands that have carried us
all that is left standing is this vastness and a mixture of hope &
joy & deep heartbreak
too many stolen from us | too early
for decades we agreed | passed down this oral understanding |
from fables to lore
in a way that not even air could replicate these words | many
infiltrators but few that live
detached from the soul of the world could even grasp the tale |
              here is where we will meet

jodya se yon promi cumplido

I have lived long out of spite and magic to see the day our
shoulders can drop, our hearts can beat, no more awaiting news
of tragedy

hoy — we have alas seen the sky have stars instead of smoke
hoy — we can see what we thought we couldn't imagine into
existence

>   weary hearts, survivors, resilient leaders, diaspora, &
>   new generations gather
>   and they still are making their way through the
>   underground cyberspace
>   AI farmers till the soil to support us—there are hands
>   that blend with the earth
>   Grandmothers, fathers, tantanns, elders, teach us what
>   it is to speak through fingertips.
>   they lead with their 3D printed canes, hover chairs &
>   overalls.

we returned to paper, burning letters, physical art and braille
so that they cannot muddle and misuse our dreams of existing
against us

our flags — secret pathways back to the homes & people &
memories waiting for us
in each place — we meet in a field of star-filled night sky like land
— Black like love and solidarity
>   *we speak renewal into existence*
The sound of wheat surrounds us &
it plentifully reminds us of abundance, sustenance, & so much
hope
orbs of those who cannot be with us physically fly all around us,
>   *affirming us along the way & offering wisdom*

together we manifest—the promise of renewal

Robots of La Resistencia keep a watchful eye for us

Indigenous, roots of people around the world span this tilled soil
garden—guiding us.
        teaching us how to listen to its messages

Variations of Brown folks speak prayers onto this bevy of seeds
        we bless renewal into existence
The sound of wheat fills the wind — a chorus of nature rebuilding
dreams are being planted, children's innocence, a father's love, a
grandmother's laugh, a mother's
wish, a teacher's lesson, lovers' expressions & secrets

        sembramos renewal into existence

smiling at my Mami Judi in her whooshing legs, followed by the
spirit of her sisters, my grandmother and aunts, supporting her
as she squats to the earth too low in her prosthesis, and they fuss.
        in this meditative movement *we nurture renewal into
existence*
This earth that is memory and new beginnings—my pup Rocco's
spirit paws and spryly walk hops—following my mother and me
(-> changed from "I") closely. Guarding and sniffing the soil.

Hundreds of miles away is the city–flying cars, smart homes, &
holotravel—but today we are ritual—we are the homes that are
attempted to be taken from us

        n'ap fe yon jaden of renewal into existence

you can hear us from anywhere if you touch your hand to any
ground, listen with your heart
renewal is coming

A Pow Wow vibrates at the beginning of the entrance of this
field, carrying our intentions in the land
Bomba y plena creates portals between the spirit realm and the
living on the left—
letting others wishing to join know where we are.

Dabke dancers fill different parts of the field
Rasin on the right – making sure how prayers reach who and
what we need.
Hymns dress many a throat, a frequency shared of possibilities
and remembering.
We commune and dance renewal into existence

The silence never came

all the clocks continued ticking
the alarms—an echo of the past
sun & sand | our becoming

The valuation of it |time| ended.

What is time when you can tap into plezi
with no one but each other to call

we arrived too used to the mindless routine of work to find US.
No delegation, no SUPERIOR, the lights off
all through the corner offices.

Silence, no. The buzzing of the bustle now translates into echoes
of US speaking,
looking at one another, too afraid to speak—we meet eyes—
converse in facial expressions
what everyone wonders inside

The news has but one host. The camera crew streams to all
devices.
This revolution was televised. This renaissance of Black and
Brown liberation is announced. We are what remains. The living.

THEY have jumped ship from eArth.

So we dance. In the streets. We go to the grocery store in what
used to be THEIR side and have

the livest Block party. Beyond Juneteenth. Beyond Martin Luther
King Day. Everyone meets
between Barack Obama and Martin Luther King Blvd &
becomes neighbors again.

Long-lost cousins connect at the function. The weary find shade
from the luxury lease buildings
overcasting the neighborhood & choose rest. Different variations
of smoke fill the air.

The children are found by the nearest elder | sit in circles
listening to stories. Grandparents
choose whether to caretake or let the village watch the baby.

It ain't all good—there's been hella beef in these streets, but
somehow the colors of separation
become a merging rainbow.

It's loud | the sun hasn't experienced so much melanin in so long
| it began to forget we are its
children. We kiss the sun | with all our grins & shy glances.

Love comes to visit us instead of counting seconds & minutes
& hours.

Family trees slowly reintroduce roots. Time becomes ~~money~~
dreams. The poets perform.
The music heads mix, the instruments play, and everyone finds
a common jazz rhythm—not quite
a cacophony, not fully symphony. But vibration.

we | been bruised & all need healing
but the minutes are minutiae

and WE reach out to each others' humanity.
some hesitantly. some silently. some angry eyes grieve a place
where they used to win. others are
in full relief. But we all stumble. needing reminders on what &
who we were before. before.
before.

as the sun sets — night falls, and the electricians find ways to
ensure we got what we need, for
now.

The silence never came, but the Joy. The joy keeps finding its
way back to us.

When the hegemonies fall

There will be a collective deep sigh.
We will rejoice, but first

We will dream, for once knowing it can be reality.

We will weep for all the weeping taken from us during survival.

We will hold hands and commune.
We will hug, we will build altars where in this lifetime everyone
comes back.

This time, we know everyone was simply waiting for home to
belong to US, and not those who
wish to pillage and overtake it

Our flags will rise as theirs burn in the ash
From the fires they lit.

Many of us may pray in gratitude.
Many of us will do rituals.
Many of us will be able to sit with our grief.
Many of us will sing all of the hymns.
Many of us will finally rest.

Many of us will need to keep fighting those trying to keep what
is dead alive.

The shades of Black, Brown, and oppressed people will fill the
streets —

queer folk will be the first to dance
as if everyone and no one is watching
this time and every time, they are met with more people joining

the men get to play with their children once again
reuniting with their sisters and wives and lovers and aunties and
mothers and brothers

we break bread, we tell strangers I love you, we apologize for
our heartaches, and still everyone
nods

we rebuild we rebuild we rebuild until our liberation is infinite,
impenetrable, sacred, and no one
dares dehumanize any of us again

But before the hegemonies fall, they force a blood ritual—call
their witches and warlocks,
Tell them to seal the deal—keep them where they've maniacally
been for centuries.

A response is given, but the cards falter, the astrology skews, &
the sky condemns.

Their desperation mounts, and murder is their response to
further grasp what never belonged.
They forgot that there are generations of spirits who have
watched them in their waking
moments.

The roots been put down low onto the groundest of grounds in
the DNA of their children's
children, tanbou vodoo has been a silent ongoing rhythm.

Their time is coming — a grasp of straws at all the culturally
stolen artifacts. You thought they
wouldn't remember who they belong to, as if your conquering
made it so. They were biding their
time. Awaiting the children and the alignment of the sky.

Your reckoning isn't what you see coming, but your condemnation.

PART IV:

Tech

Russell Nichols

Girls Flying High

We regret to inform you that we currently do not have gravity boots in your size.

The message pops up a week before the start of the fall semester. The school rush-ordered a custom-made pair, but now you have to wait to move in. Being already twenty-some-odd years behind, what's an extra few days? All that means is you won't be able to lay low like you'd planned to.

"Damn, you musta got held back hella times," says one of the girls on your first day.

"I thought you was the substitute for real," says another.

"Okay, Granny!" says a third.

The Bessie Coleman Flying School for Girls has no age limit. The floating academy hovers four thousand feet in wide-open Texas airspace. You and your thirty-nine-year-old self have every right to be up here.

The school offers you a private room, the one reserved for guest speakers. You decline. You'll sleep in the dorm with the other twenty-four girls, thank you. That last bunk next to the restroom is yours. Living with an abusive ex taught you how to hold your breath for long periods. The constant flushing, you tell yourself in the dark, is nothing but gusts of wind.

The first couple weeks consist of lectures and holographic diagrams. The main flight instructor, Ms. Jamie, has flown to space twice before. "Lady Afronaut," the girls call her. She teaches about drag and uplift and the principles of aerodynamics, which you already learned as a single mother.

On the way to class, you pass the advanced girls headed to the launchpad. Their golden bootstraps mean they can fly without permission. During the lunch hour, you eat grilled chicken tacos with a squeeze of lime, wrapped in whole-grain tortillas, topped with fresh pico de gallo. Reminds you of Taco Tuesdays back home, which makes you think of your three kids—all out of the house finally, making some kind of life for themselves. You put yours on hold for them, but they'll never understand that. Catch-up is a lonely game to play.

Standing at a porthole, you watch the advanced girls take flight. Watch them leap. Watch them spread their arms wide, tuck them in to dive. Watch them glide, melanated skin making the sun blush. Watch their hair—locs and box braids and extensions—flapping behind them, stroked by windfingers. You cut all yours off after your last breakup.

By week four, the digs have died down. Still, you keep to yourself mostly. The girls think you're overly serious—or as twelve-year-old Anila put it: "Way too heavy to ride the wind."

Is she right?

You remember yourself then. Fully grown at twelve. Couldn't nobody tell you nothing. How unburdened you were. Unmarked by the hands of those who tried and tried to keep you grounded for posterity's sake. By those who called you out your name and those who didn't call you back. Acceptance felt worse than rejection because how could you trust anyone who accepted you? When your kids would say they loved you, you wondered where they learned to lie.

But those days are beneath you. Among the clouds, you're in your defiant era. You and your thirty-nine-year-old self came to this school to defy, defy, defy. To reject every idea held over you. Every word hurled against you. To let go of the longing to be longed for—a desperation that drove you into the arms of weighty men who looked you in your eyes and said: "Baby, I'm tryna hold you down."

And you let them.

Because at least you were being held.

Ms. Jamie read a quote in class, something about how a bird doesn't land on a branch because it trusts the branch—it trusts its wings. But what becomes of the broken-winged?

By week sixteen, the girls had gotten used to you. During breakfast, Anila comes to stand beside you at your porthole. Together, you watch the girls outside.

Out of the blue, she asks: "How come you just now learning to fly?"

The question flits in the space between you. How do you explain to this girl how scary it feels to surrender yourself to nature? How, after years in certain environments, trust is known to erode? How tiny cracks in confidence, left unchecked, can grow into chasms you're not sure how to get over?

These are things that you can't explain; only endure.

You look into her brown eyes. So wide and unweary, so full of wonder. Unweighted by the chorus of inner voices screaming: *Nobody sees you!* And the poisons you partook to drown it out.

Even as you envy her innocence, you remind yourself you're in your defiant era. You look outside again. You watch the girls flying high. Watch them spread their arms wide, tuck them in to dive. Watch them glide, melanated skin making the sun blush. True, they know how to soar but don't yet understand the profoundly painful forces of propulsion. What's flight without gravity?

You walk away from the porthole with a defiant strut.

"Hold up," Anila calls, trailing behind you. "Where you going?"

At the launchpad, you breathe in and let the atmosphere fill you. Like liberation in your lungs.

"Your bootstraps aren't golden." Anila looks around, on edge. "You can't fly without permission."

You switch off your custom-made gravity boots, look her in her eyes and say: "Watch me."

Esteban Gaspar Silva

Aztlán.exe

The digital manifestation of the mythical homeland will be
voracious in quantum architecture
The seven caves will provide a source code based on the
technological adaptation of the mystical
Statues will be erected not in the devotion of people but
rather as theoretical pillars of progress
Salvation will be re-formatted as a communal effort rather
than that of the unknown

ARMONIZADORES_XOCHIMILCA
operation: Frequency Harmonization Network
　　IF (corporate_frequencies detected)
　　　THEN: activate_ancient_resonance + purify_waves
　　WHILE (digital_cleansing_active)
　　　MAINTAIN: sacred_frequency_protection
END_PROTOCOL

//Archaic systems of governance are null//
//Archaic visions of social structures are null//
//Archaic delineation of borders are null//

TEJEDORAS_DIGITALES_TLAHUICA
operation: Memory Textile Network
    IF (colonial_data detected)
        THEN: weave_counter_narrative + encrypt_in_patterns
    WHILE (community_stories_active)
        PROTECT: ancestral_code_weaving
    IF (pattern_strength > surveillance_capacity)
        THEN: distribute_resistant_textiles
END_PROTOCOL

We hold each function accountable for the sacred
engineering in building the infinite
Systems of digital healing will be administered through
open-source conviction and reverence
A spiritual firewall will be deployed through community
bringing forth an Aeon of Xolotl
Eternity lies at the forefront of conflict, tradition is but a
guideline, not a dogma

CRONISTAS_CAOS_CHALCA
operation: Temporal Sovereignty Network
    IF (standard_time detected)
        THEN: deploy_local_time + disrupt_synchronization
    WHILE (colonial_calendar active)
        MAINTAIN: indigenous_temporal_systems
    IF (time_sovereignty threatened)
        THEN: activate_chaos_protocols
END_PROTOCOL

Resource scarcity shall be rendered as a bygone semblance
of governmental failure
Alchemic frequencies cleanse each digital space in
observance of a democratic hyperlink

//Education will prevail//
//Autonomy will be restored//
//Paths will be unfolded//

MERCENARIOS_MEMORIA_TLAXCALTECA
operation: Memory Preservation
    IF (historic_erasure detected)
        THEN: activate_memory_backup + protect_archives
    IF (corporate_deletion attempted)
        THEN: deploy_memory_guardians
END_PROTOCOL

The Future Will Be Indigenx://
[Tech]nochtitlán Will Rise

Superintelligence Speaks in Náhuatl

Uncompiled / Xixini (to scatter/disperse)
"Uncomxixinid" - Rhizomatic in nature, democratic, autonomous

Network / Nelhuayotl (roots/origins)
"Netlhuayork " - Ancestors guide our collective decisions, histories set the foreground

Open Source / Huehuetlatolli (ancient words/wisdom)
"Huehuetlatolli Source" - Repository of elder knowledge, ever-changing, fluid

Algorithm / Tlalli (earth)
"Tlalgorithm" - Earth code serving as a framework for integration and communication

Electronic / Omeyocan (place of duality)
"Omeyectronic" - quantum computations in the realm of duality, a balance with nature

Sovereign / Cemanahuatl (the world, universe)
"Cemanavernty" - aligning with cosmic first and foremost, respect for the inherent value of life

Matrix / Tecpatl (flint knife)
"Tecpatrix" - dissection of the ceremonial dataspace, tools of regenerative network protection

Encryption / Teotl (divine energy/force)
"Encrypteotl" - divine hardwiring of safety for the needs of each community

Protocol / Ollin (movement/motion)
"Protollin" - movement according to the needs of liberation, will, and self-actualization

Distributed / Tequitl (tribute/community work)
"Distributequitl" - community-based data distribution, collaboration, and transparency

The Death of Tlal[tech]uhtli

The technological was severed from a depiction of the sublime
Apocalyptic fear subsides after several iterations

To be ripped into an act of creation forsakes the consequences
Mistakes shape a concept of time that exists on a quantum realm

To be endlessly hungry feels like the very essence of life
The triumph of such cruelty brings about the positioning of
landscape

Each rough hand upholds a vestige of the world we know
Each mountain becomes a reminder of violence

Now sacrifice keeps the sixth mass extinction from devouring
the life we know
Despite our desperate pleas for mercy from further red flag
warnings

The machine has demanded a debt of life in its most essential
form
Server farms underline a need for solutions at a pace that is
unbound

Understanding events through Teotl rather than sequential
causation
Our chronological reliance has rendered a world of scarcity

Considering cosmic cycles rather than linear projections
Salvation continues to shapeshift into a tide of furtherance

To organize information into taxonomies of sacred distinctions
Is to evolve beyond our understanding of the profane

Let silicon return to sacred sand as binary transforms in analog
predictions
Let each circuit board bloom with marigolds answering our
timed-out queries
Let our dreams ignite a dawn of possibility as every pixel burns
with memories of forever

PART V:

Death

Lisa Bradley

Haunted

A haunting is when events become unmoored from time.
These events bob on the surface of a certain kind
of consciousness, evident to mediums, seers, shamans.
They flicker, echo, and repeat in space, accruing, often,
an imbrication of meanings that overlap like dragon scales.
They grow denser and denser with each iteration 'til tales
evolve around them and even the most obtuse can see
these ghostly motions—unless blinkered by rationality.

Our world is haunted.

We have been shuffled from our rightful place in history,
our Aztec ancestors both marks and money card
in a game of three-card monte that links our story
to ancient civilizations that rose and fell hard—
Egyptian, Roman, Atlantean—peoples real and faux
who disappeared because they had to, ceding all
to the "superior" race, which endeavors not to know
they are the force and reason for our empire's fall.

Our land is haunted.

But no civilization can be completely overpainted.

Strong lines bleed through and we are always engineering
new ways to detect the pentimento. So
Aztecs exist in three locations: in the antiquated
BCEs, the 15th and 16th centuries, even appearing
in the here and now, if you hear our Nahuatl.
We are the inconvenient message in a bottle
that keeps returning to the shore.

This border is haunted.

We keep being shoved from the timeline.
How many times have they thrown us back?
There's no room in the Great Depression's
Dustbowl drama for the million displaced Mexicans,
about half of us US citizens, who were "repatriated"
under Hoover. Nor does the portrait of poodle skirts
and sock hops in the '50s permit
even a hidden figure representing
over a million deportees in Eisenhower's Operation
Wetback. The president of hope,
Obama, also served as Deporter-in-Chief
and caged children, ruined the lives of more migrants
than any other American president, though Trump
is giving him a run for his money.

I am haunted.

Our erasure keeps happening and we hold
two versions of truth in our minds at all times.
What might arise if we tangled the lines,
if time wrinkled enough for hauntings to fold
back into history? Would we permit its rhymes?
Is a tesseract justice or mere evidence of crimes?

Pessimism plagues my thoughts and stops me cold.

I am a haunting.

Perhaps I prefer to be outside time
twitchy as a flipbook animation seen
from the corner of your evasive eye.
Perhaps it is for the best that I've been

let loose on the sea of eternity
and, silent, may creep up, erupt
in your rivers, my spontaneity
engulfing all of your corrupt

crafts and reminding you
how flimsy they are,
apt, when faced with truth,
to melt like paper stars

in surf. Spritely, I'm not locked
in your goosestep chronology.
I can shapeshift, unblocked
by your biased ontology.

My people and I are worthy,
whether or not you agree,
and we'll keep appearing
until you're forced to see

Us
in every era.

Molara Wood

The Stranger

"Death calls the mọ̀lẹ́bí together," Ikúòmọlà said as he lay dying, on a bed that sat in somewhat incongruous majesty in the drawing room of his country mansion.

"We wish you wouldn't talk like this," said one among us.

Ikúòmọlà gave a weak shrug. "When it's your time to go, it's your time to go."

The family had moved his bed down a floor from his bedroom to the drawing room for this fated denouement, to better accommodate the large number of us present.

Ikúòmọlà raised his head a fraction from pillows that propped up his upper half, listening for a sound that rumbled as an undercurrent to our conversation. A shadow flitted across his face.

We turned to the source of the rumbling, a diminutive figure who wept with the low drone of a mutant bee and sniffled constantly. We had all exchanged greetings amongst ourselves and with Ikúòmọlà's spouse and offspring upon our arrival. We had not noticed the entrance of this lachrymose one, but there he was, crumbled in an ungainly heap on a pouf in a corner, face down, oblivious of our stares.

"How did you all get my summons?" Ikúòmọlà asked as he settled back down.

"An announcement on the radio," someone said.

"I saw it in the family WhatsApp group, our branch of the family tree," said another.

"A huge family tree," came a voice from the back. Many of us nodded and exchanged glances to signal our agreement.

"Visiting your home for the first time, too," said a woman who had flown in from overseas to heed the call.

"Death calls the mọ̀lẹ́bí together," Ikúòmọlà said.

*

The four boys were on the farm during Practical Agric when they discovered a crack in the wall that encircled their remote boarding school. The school sat at the edge of a dense forest.

"You know what this means?" asked Ikúòmọlà.

"We can sneak out of school whenever we like?"

"Even better, we can go into the forest itself!" Ikúòmọlà poked an elbow into his friend's side. He thought himself the cleverest of the boys. The Three Stooges, he called his friends, based on characters they saw in a film once.

With their cutlasses and hoes, the boys dug into the wall and widened the crack, big enough to let them through one at a time. They left tall yam plants undisturbed near the spot, for concealment. The crack in the wall was their secret.

*

Ikúòmọlà addressed his kin in the drawing room. "I called you all here to hear my final words, and to bear witness to my last will as spoken by me concerning my wealth, who gets what as regards my properties, art collection, the lot."

On the wall above the carved mahogany headboard hung the most prized artwork in his collection: a small woven piece, provenance unknown, which his eldest child stood to inherit.

"Perhaps we can introduce ourselves," said the woman from overseas, "since many of us are meeting for the first time."

"Good idea," said a tall, spindly man, who described himself and his two companions as old schoolfriends of the ailing man. He had sent for them, too.

We each stood up and introduced ourselves. The tiny weeping one, when it came to his turn, seemed lost in his misery. He was robed head to toe in a thick bark-patterned fabric that left his face in shadow. We skipped him. He droned on.

"I have lived a good life," Ikúòmọlà began, when the introductions were over. "I have taken chances and beaten unimaginable odds. I want, finally, to talk about my greatest triumph, which in truth is the source of the immense fortune that has made my home its abode."

He paused, as the droning and sniffling grew more insistent from the strange one's corner. The mood was catching; some of us fished out tissues to dab at the corners of our eyes.

Ikúòmọlà turned to his old school friends. "To you, The Three Stooges, friends of my youth, a confession: we made a pact once, many years ago, but I alone saw it through."

*

"What if we go into the forest and don't come back?" asked one of the boys, spindly, tall for his age.

"What if we encounter goblins and monsters, or get torn apart by wild animals?" said the second boy, who walked with a slight stoop.

Ikúòmọlà's eyes glinted. "What if we see an Egbére?"

"The roaming spirit of the woods! I've heard of such," said Spindly.

"Egbére is a depressing sight, I hear; snotty-nosed, crying through the forest," Stoop said.

"Do they even exist?" The third boy scrunched up his pockmarked face.

Spindly piped up. "Is it true what they say about the mat?"

"Egbére's mat? We'll find out, won't we?" Ikúòmọlà cackled. "And when we do, we're set up for life!"

"Promise to share?" asked one boy.

"Promise to share," they all chorused.

They hatched a plan to sneak out to the forest the following Saturday, when the school would be busy with Founders Day activities in the main hall and no one would notice their absence.

*

The Three Stooges looked at themselves and back at the man on the bed. To their open mouths, their unspoken question, Ikúòmọlà gave a nod.

"No!" Spindly blurted out.

"Yes..." Ikúòmọlà said.

"But we were thwarted, caught by Ogunji the hunter," said Stoop.

"And he dragged us back to the school by our ears," Pockmark said. "'Respect the forest' – Ogunji kept saying. I'll never forget."

"Nor I." Spindly nodded. "The hunter said we were greedy and unkind. 'Your mat of riches, Egbére's sole inheritance from his mother' – he scolded us. We were shamefaced."

"We were in big, big trouble when we got to the headmaster's office." Stoop stuck out an index finger towards the bed. "And you, Ikúòmọlà. You were expelled because you skipped the punishment."

"How could I forget? I jumped out of the headmaster's window and stole into the forest." Ikúòmọlà turned his face away. "A rendezvous awaited me, you see. A date with destiny."

*

He heard the creature before he saw it. A lugubrious emission that suffused the trees and echoed all around. Ikúòmọlà had trudged through thick jungle for hours, sustaining scratches to his arms from nettles and thorns. But he kept his energies up, spurred on by the certainty that, if he could prise Egbére's treasure from its hand, he'd never lack. The school could do as it pleased after that. As the mournful droning drew near, he measured his breathing and focused, even as the creature's wailing tore at his soul. Stepping gingerly on the underbrush, he came to a small clearing swathed in mist and sun rays slanting fiercely through the tree canopy. And there in the radiating sunbeam was the silhouette shuffling this way, feet leaden with sorrow, unaware of Ikúòmọlà's presence, until the mat was snatched from its hands.

Ikúòmọlà turned and bolted, sprinting faster than he did on the school's athletic tracks on Inter House Sports day, hardly noticing the bushes and branches that lashed and tore at him as he fled. The Egbére gave chase but lost ground. And even as Ikúòmọlà emerged from the forest, he could still hear the droning in every sinew of his body, a woeful lament breathed into the very air, into his ears.

"Human!! You have robbed me of my comfort!! I will find you! The riches you seek shall crumble to dust!!"

*

Ikúòmọlà coughed feebly, and we leaned forward in our seats with anxious faces. A nurse dabbed at his mouth with a tissue, felt his forehead.

The Three Stooges looked wide-eyed at their old friend, their mouths agape.

"That's right," Ikúòmọlà said with a thin smile. "The Egbére's mat made me rich. And I have lived with the terror of that hideous noise, those words he breathed into me, and the quiet fear that he might find me. But I overcame him. I know that now. I won."

"We plighted a troth, and you broke the pact," Pockmark spoke in almost a whisper, eyes narrowed.

"You didn't share," said Stoop.

"And Ogunji's caution, what about that?" Spindly looked around as though addressing us all.

Ikúòmọlà opened his mouth to speak, but he only spluttered. His coughs grew into a fit.

But hardly anyone noticed by then. The woven art on the wall was glimmering, incandescent, burning bright, like flickering flames.

"Like a globular star cluster bursting into life," said one of us, who once got A1 in WAEC O' Level Physics but did nothing with it.

The droning and weeping accelerated and expanded and grew into deafening decibels, and our hands flew to our ears. We cowered as the small figure rose from his corner and loomed over us all, his cover-cloth flapping like a magician's cape caught in the howling wind. He gestured expansively towards the woven artwork. Sparks burst forth from the piece, and the drawing room grew thick with mist.

We all seemed to hear the hoary cry deep within our beings.

"Human! You robbed me of my comfort! The riches you sought shall crumble to dust!"

The stranger took his leave in the sunbeam of his own conjuring, and none knew in which direction he went. As the mist dissipated, the mọlẹ́bí rose to find Ikúòmọlà lifeless on the bed.

The woven piece was gone from the wall, and Ikúòmọlà's mansion was refabricating itself into thick forest all around us.

Shaira Chaer

"Rice Water"

Every morning was the same. The clinking chain link of the cistern, and the buckets dumping water into smaller containers for the kitchen, chickens and bath woke me up before the first rooster's crowing. By the time I'd get out of bed, squinty-eyed after a restless night (I refused to sleep with a mosquito net/el *mosquitero* and had welts/*hinchazones* on my eyelids, physical evidence to my stubbornness), my aunt had already mopped most of the house. I could always expect to see her on the front porch/*la marquesina*, spreading water across the floor with her splintered broom. I think that broom was older than I was.

The scent of Café Santo Domingo, followed by the fresh smell of newly delivered *pan de agua*, filled the air, mixing and mingling. The loaves of bread beckoned to be cut open, a delicious tomb for butter and *queso de papa*.

"*Dormiste bien, mi amor?*" Did you sleep well, my dear?

"*Si, tía.*" Half a lie.

"*Si no te picaban en los ojos, te dijera que te pusiera un poco de mentol. A ti siempre te comen viva.*" If they hadn't bitten you in the eyes, I'd tell you to put some menthol on it. They always eat you alive, tía Chucha would say, bucktooth teeth stained with her two shots of café, gearing up for a third. The mosquito bites looked worse than they felt after popping my eyes open.

As a kid, my parents spent what little they had on a one-way ticket from the Bronx to Santo Domingo for the summer break. Unlike the lack of routine back home, mornings at Mama Colombina's were always spent like this—waking up to chores, an early breakfast, espresso I couldn't drink but enjoyed all the same, bare feet on a cold, damp floor, wicker chair rocking back and forth, scratching at new and couple-day-old mosquito bites.

The sun dances at the back of the house now, spilling over the openings of the makeshift chicken coop. Mama picks through rice kernels, leaving some of the rejects out for the birds, chicks, and hens to peck at. Josefina, the stray black cat who made a home for herself in the coop, watches from afar. The chicken coop is more decorative than functional, a remnant of my uncle's gambling and cock fighting days. Now, it serves as a home for a couple of chicks and Josefina's litter of kittens.

"'*Cion, mama*." I'd plant a kiss where her hair met her temple. Asking for an elder's blessing is a cultural ritual demonstrating respect, something Dominicans are heavy on, but it's a closed, bottom-up practice. I learned that lesson from her daughter, my mother, who inherited her tyranny from her father, my grandfather, Mama's husband. I never met the bastard (he died almost 20 years before I was born) and have only seen his steely, unkind face in two photos. She never talked badly about him, but that was the thing about it all—she *never* talked about him. Judging by the lack of family photos with him, I imagine Mama was happy the day he died. To be free from him, to have reign over this tiny kingdom they built for themselves, to choose how to spend her days, unafraid.

"Dios te bendiga, mi hija." The teeth spared from osteoporosis revealed themselves in her smile, also stained with espresso. I'm not sure a woman who bore seven kids knew what sleeping in meant, but she seemed well-rested despite her aches and pains. While taking her daily walk on Avenida Nicolas de Ovando, a motorcyclist ran her over, an accident that ended her autonomy. It took two surgeries to repair the damage. She stopped going for walks. Her hair thinned. Her joints were swollen and tender. Her varicose veins looked angry, like lightning striking across her legs. You couldn't tell she was in pain; she refused help, and her cane collected dust in the corner of her bedroom. Despite this, she viewed her internalized ableism as a strength and leveraged that martyrdom over her children, grandchildren, and great-grandchildren in harmful ways. That's a story for some other time.

I was a relatively still sleeper, so I was allowed to share a bed with her. She lived in a small two-bedroom home with a massive living room, a stuffy kitchen, and about a half acre of land split between a patch of grass in the front of the house, a driveway, and a cement-paved yard with a few trees. Mama's cherry tree was overshadowed by her guava tree, which provided a canopy over the entire house and much-needed shade during the hottest months. Her room was at the front of the house, so the world was her alarm clock. She could hear everything from bed—every neighbor's passing conversation, every rooster crowing, every vendor yelling, *"Platano grande a 5 peso,'"* (Big plantains for five bucks) or *"Tengo yame, yautia, mango, cereza, guineo,"* (I've got yams, malanga, mango, cherries, bananas) through a makeshift bullhorn plugged into their stereo.

I would always pretend to be asleep just to watch her in the mornings. She'd gingerly sit up, using the makeshift hospital railing as an assist, her lacquered pearly pink nails glinting in the early morning light. After shuffling around in the bathroom, she'd return to bed, staring at herself in the mirror my late grandfather purchased. The mirror was almost blue, with yellow tinges and brown spots, aging like she had been. And yet, as though the mirror itself copied her movements, or by her talent, she would slowly pull every bobby pin out of her hair, one at a time. She grabbed her reliable, too-old comb to part and brush her hair sideways, pulling her short black and grey hair into a low bun with the ease and precision of a ballet dancer. Maybe it wasn't a mirror at all. Perhaps it was a portal for her, one only she could see and travel through to whichever segment of her life made her the happiest. And maybe what I saw was her body double in the land of the living, responsible only for making sure her morning routine proceeded without a hitch. No one would suspect a thing.

Every morning, I got a glimpse of her ritual, and it became my ritual, too—the ritual of watching. Watching and wishing I was the brush, the bristles, separating each strand into delicate waves, massaging the thoughts in her head, her mental checklist, her memories.

At around 9 am, I would sit in the yard with her after our *café and pan de agua* breakfast to help her pick through rice. When we finished, I rinsed the rice again and watched Mama bless the pot with water, salt, and avocado oil. We moved on to peeling stalks of *guandules*. Sometimes, I'd eat the seeds inside, and she'd laugh.

"*Espérate, eso es para ahorita. ¿Te lo vas a comer crudo?*" Wait, those are for later. Are you going to eat them raw?

Picky eater as I was, I'd reply, "*Son bueno así,*" making a scene of munching on just one little bean. *They're good just the way they are.*

I haven't been back to the Dominican Republic in over a decade. There is a laundry list of reasons why (*1. The Dominican state was a manifestation of neocolonialism, 2. Geopolitical tensions between Quisqueya and Ayiti are textbook examples of why there is no such thing as a "two-state solution," 3. The state-sanctioned violence against Haitian kin, 4. The state-sanctioned abuse against women, girls, and trans and queer kin, 5. My abuser is family, 6. I let my passport expire and haven't replaced it, et cetera*), but Mama died before I could plan a return trip. The last time we saw each other, I was in the throes of breaking out of an abusive relationship, and she was in the early stages of dementia. We didn't speak to each other very much during my visit, but she called for me the morning before I flew back to New York City.

"*¿Puedes bajar el volumen?*" she gestured to the remote, instructing me to lower the volume on her afternoon game show. The silence was palpable, broken only by the private symphony of my heart thumping away.

"*¿Necesitas algo mas?*" I asked, wondering if she mistook me for a cousin of mine, or some other family member who spent half of their life taking turns caring for her.

With earth-shattering clarity, she said, "*Amor que duele no es amor. Ese hombre te va dejar si no te mata primero.*" Love isn't supposed to hurt. That man is going to leave you unless he kills you beforehand.

But love *is* pain, I wanted to say. I saw it play out between my mother and father, between neighbors, between the cordiality tinged with rage from people who were once each other's forever. And how did she know about that anyway? I thumbed the Rolodex of suspects in my head, relatives who spilled whatever tidbits my mother found out about my private life carelessly and loud enough for Mama to put the pieces together. I could only nod my head. "Okay, mama." She outstretched a hand to mine, and I stared at the wrinkles between her knuckles to keep my composure, a tapestry of grace and wisdom.

"*Siempre me recuerdo de ti como niña. Había veces cuando me preguntabas si estabas soñando, si era verdad que estabas aquí conmigo, cuánto te encantaba Santo Domingo y cuánto extrañabas la mesedora,*" she shakingly raised her arms to imitate me, childlike wonder, and maybe tears, twinkling in her eyes. I could have sobbed, but I let it out as a half-laugh, half-groan. Mama remembered me—the memories I held onto so dearly, the summers spent at her house. I smiled, remembering her in that old creaky rocking chair, the very one I loved to curl up in with a book when she wasn't using it, basking in her scent of baby powder, jabon de cuaba, and off-brand hair gel.

"*No te olvides. Te quiero mucho.*" She let me go, took the remote back from me, and put the volume back up, her body relaxing back into an almost comatose state. Her last words held me together after my relationship came to a tumultuous end, and returned when I decided to spin the block with the same man, almost getting myself killed in the process. The memory of waking up in a jolt from the passenger seat of a moving car, swerving off the road, and lunging at the steering wheel to prevent a crash became part of my postpartum intrusive thoughts, worsened by lack of sleep.

And maybe that was why I dreamt about her ten years later. Maybe I conjured her up after pumping breastmilk for a fussy newborn, crying and reflecting on the failures of my twenties. I silently prayed to the ancestors: "Whoever is listening, I call upon you. Remind me that this weight is not mine alone to carry."

After lying back down (removed: "after putting my head back") on the pillow, I saw her waiting for me in a hotel lobby in the city.

Colombina had never been to the States before. She never got on a plane, either. She stayed in that little house on Calle 34-A in Cristo Rey before the Great Forgetting began (*I looked at your casita on Google Maps, and it's not green anymore. It's bronze and black and brick. The hibiscus are gone.*). I always wondered what happened to Mama's furniture before they sold her house. Did the old mirror, her chairs, the chicken coop, and all her keepsakes and mementos end up in a dump?

Colombina wore all black, hair slicked back into her signature style. But she looked younger, like the sepia photograph that used to hang in her bedroom. She sat on what looked like a velvet chaise lounge, facing away from me. As if on autopilot, I adjusted the pillows behind the small of her back. "I'm fine," she replied in English. *¡Mamá nunca aprendió a hablar inglés!* What is this?

I insisted, fluffing anyway because I cannot finish a task before I can complete it.

"*Mira, te enseño,*" she said, getting up seamlessly.

I watched her, handing her a coffee and a grilled cheese I don't remember holding. She looked at it, then me, with disdain. "That bread doesn't even look real, and the cheese? I can tell it's flavorless."

She took it, bit down, (*removed: "and took a bite"*) and mumbled, "Gringos and their day-old bread," crunching away.

"If it isn't good, I can get something else," I said, and she grabbed my wrist lightly, buttered fingers leaving greasy prints.

"It's okay, just sit with me."

We sipped our coffee, hip to hip on the chaise, people-watching. The silence felt like an embrace.

"So what is this place?" I questioned.

"You asked for a sign," she said, smiling sadly.

"Yes, I needed to remember what home felt like. It's such a strange concept to me, now that I have the baby, and what feels like a new body. I also..." I shifted around in my seat, adding quietly, "I wanted to remember you. I stopped to think about you because my first kid wears me down, but that's nothing, 'cause you had seven! And for some reason, I couldn't remember your face."

It was true. I only saw a remnant when I tried to picture Mama. It was shaped like her, sure, but made of static.

She hummed in understanding. "Sometimes photographs aren't enough."

Lip trembling, I trepidated, tracing circles on her hand with my fingertips: "Are you really here right now?"

"Well, technically, *you're* here. This is an in-between place. I'm not really sure how to explain it to you, but I can't tell why you chose to put us in a hotel lobby. *¿Quieres ir a casa?*"

I grabbed her hand, suddenly clean and free of stale bread and watered-down coffee. "Wait, wha—um...how exactly does this work?"

She squeezed my hand in return, and suddenly, we were in her house, in her backyard—chicks pecking at the pebbled rice, Josefina lounging lazily in the sun, Mama sifting through rice water. Now my hand was buttery, the other holding already-opened *pan de agua*, *queso de papa* melting inside.

"We never really leave the places we love, you know. They are always available to us here." Mama tapped a wet finger to her temple, thumping once, twice, three times. A swirling, dreamlike portal opened, a gentle song inviting me to choose this existence or another. I peered into the mist and looked down to see myself in bed, contorted under sheets but unmoving, possessed by a rare, deep sleep.

"You can go back home, or you can stay here with me a little longer. *¡Y no sé tú, pero yo estoy disfrutando de este aguacero!*"

On cue, the heavens opened to—at first—a drizzle, then a downpour of rain. The chickens raced each other into the coop, Josefina's fluffy black tail following close behind like a shepherd protecting her flock. Mama took the bowl of rice into the kitchen and reemerged with a catlike grin.

"Did you know it's *guayaba* season?" The smell of sweet, musky guava hit me immediately as I looked up, squinting through the downpour. Hurricane Georges had cracked the guava tree into pieces, but there it was, more lush than I remembered. After a double take, its small flowers bloomed into fruit.

"Can you climb up to get them?" she challenged me, already racing down the path to the roof, the best way to grab a branch and pull the fruit out.

"*¿Estás segura?* We have to be careful," I called after her, laughing nervously. She was already halfway up the ladder, with more vigor than I had seen on her best days in the land of the living.

The clouds parted as she reached into the tree, plucking the first guayaba, green and dewy. I dove into my pocket for a knife I didn't know was there until I felt its weight, and she winked as she tossed the fruit to me. She reached back into the branch as I grabbed another guava. The first bite was as sweet as I remembered. We giggled in satisfaction.

She curtseyed, extending her skirt longer and longer until we had a surface to sit over the cold, wet cement. The rain hadn't ended yet, but the sunbeams were already drying our clothes.

"*Se esta casando la bruja*," we (removed: "both") sang in unison.

I swallowed down the lump in my throat with a fleshy, tangy swallow. "How can something so bitter be so sweet?" I asked as she moved closer to me, until we sat hip to hip again.

"I'm guessing you don't mean the fruit," she said with a curious shrug. "*¿Así es la vida, no?* Good today, shitty tomorrow. But you're not looking for answers."

I took another bite, trying to slow down my chewing to bask in the moment. "No, I guess not," I mumbled, looking down at my lap, the knife gleaming up at me with the light of the full sun, unrestricted by clouds.

"*¿Y entonces?*" she asked, pushing me playfully. I took one good look at her. Her crinkled eyes, her dimples, the moles on her neck, her hair, still somehow perfectly slicked back into her signature low bun. It felt like I was watching a flower bloom, like the hibiscus she would grow, prune, and brew into sweet tea. A *lagarto* cozied up close to me, scheming over the guava carcasses. I didn't know what to say.

In this place, death was all around us—the house that no longer existed, the backyard animals, the *guayaba* tree, the other details I couldn't remember anymore. But the peace I felt hummed so vibrantly I thought I would burst. I had been missing this feeling for 10 years, a timely reminder of what mattered to me as a child; one of the few bright spots in my life was in those quotidian summers with Mama.

As if reading, she replied, "That's the point of this place. It's an oasis for remembering. The people you love who aren't alive anymore exist in the cracks of these liminal spaces, waiting for their kids and kin to visit them."

I stopped stripping my last bit of fruit with my teeth and swallowed hard. "So you just wait forever? Doesn't it get lonely?"

She laughed. "That's for the living, to keep you all humble. I can go anywhere, anytime, and be as young or as old as I'd like. I can visit the people I love who are across this plane. There's no such thing as time or pain or loneliness here. It just *is*, and we just *are*. Nothing more or less than that."

After gorging ourselves on too many of those delectable miracle stone fruits, we returned to the house. I prepped and set the *greca* for Mama, grabbed tía Chucha's old broom, and poured leftover rice water, fresh rainwater, and blue Mistolin on the floor before sweeping. (Rewritten from: "It feels like ages") Ages seemed to pass like this as we cleaned, hummed, and laughed at nothing.

Mama watched me from her rocking chair for what felt like infinity, and as my movements began to slow, she said, "It's almost time for you to wake up, isn't it?"

I nodded. "It feels like pushing through a strong current with my hands. *Como olas en la playa*," I finally finished. Back in the land of the living, I felt the sun peeking through my curtains, a scene I watched through the portal she left open in the yard.

"*¿Cuándo volverás?*" she asked. When will you come back?

My lack of an answer felt cruel after an afternoon of time travel and impossibilities, but she didn't ask again, extending a hand to place the broom back by the door. "Here, I'll help you. I've seen how it works with your mom. She tends to fight going back when it's time for her."

She comes here, too? There was so much I wanted to say, but the weight of my tongue made speaking a herculean effort. (rewrite:) I wished she could see inside my mind, see all the regret I carried about not being able to come back before she died, about not being the one to clean her grave on her birthday or Mother's Day or during the holidays she loved so much.

"Yes, I know. I see everything that happens, *como telenovelas*. And no, I'm not mad at you. I am proud of you. Even on your worst days, you're doing a great job. Try not to forget that, okay?"

She planted a kiss on my cheek, and we started our trek back. When she realized I couldn't walk above a glacial pace, she opted to carry me like an infant, stopping in front of the portal.

"You'll go back like nothing happened. You might not remember how to get back here, but I'll be waiting when you do. Josefina will be here too, and the chickens, and the fruit..."

Her voice, still running through the list, started to trail off.

In awe and sadness, I mustered my remaining strength (rewritten from: "the strength I have left to say"). "*Te quiero*," I said, an echo of her last words to me.

Before I registered what was happening, she pushed me back into my body and faded, slowly, into nothingness.

Nick "squidpizza" Cuevas

A Dog and Her Boy

Call her Dog.

Nobody calls her Dog, of course. Nobody speaks to the dogs that roam the city streets,

Except perhaps to yell at them.

Call him Boy.

That is not his name, of course, but Dog doesn't understand names. He gives Her corncobs and week-old slices of deli ham sometimes.

His mother tells him not to. That the Dog will hang around.

Grow complacent.

And anyway, those ones bite. Everyone knows those ones bite.

But He doesn't listen, and sneaks Dog even more little treats.

She grows complacent.

She follows Him around when He roams the streets, putting up posters or spraying paint on concrete walls.

His friends give her a wide berth. Pit bulls bite. Everyone knows pit bulls bite. But She follows anyway. Not expecting a treat,

(not that She would turn one down, hint-hint)

But because that is what dogs do.

They follow their Masters.

...

And then one day, the streets are crowded. Signs are raised, people shout, windows are smashed. Dog does not understand. It is beyond Her understanding.

But people shout, and Boy is pushed down onto the hot asphalt of the street, And a monster swings at him.

And Dog knows what to do. It is encoded in her very DNA. Dogs defend their masters. And she does the only thing she knows to do. She moves like tan lightning, honed in on her target like a swooping eagle.

She bites. And bites. and bites. and bites.

Even when Her paw is crushed under the heavy boot of the Thing She has Her jaws clamped on, She bites.

Even when She is kicked, and hit with sticks, and sprayed with chemicals that burn Her eyes like fire, She bites.

She does not let go.

Even as everything goes black, She does not let go.

...

Many years pass.

The Boy, now a Man, keeps a flash drive in his desk. Dog was buried in the backyard of a house that no longer exists. The drive is a memory, in more than one sense.

He gets a call from an associate. He listens intently and cries. "Thank you," He says. "Thank you."

He takes the subway to the lab. It is a clean, white place. Sterile. And yet, there is noise. The sound of dogs barking.

The Man hands the flash drive to a stranger, an expert in animal neurology. She has grand plans. To her, this is a trial run, a test, to see if she can change the world.

To Him, it is the world. It is the sun and the moon and the stars.

The process takes hours. The data is old now. Encoded shortsightedly for programs written ten years ago. How foolish of the programmers to not see into the future.

The body is a special order. Nobody had asked for a pit bull yet. So it had to be designed. That was sorted out months ago, though. The brain is another matter.

...

Dog wakes up confused. She has no idea how sophisticated Her new body is. It is beyond Her understanding.

But the Man does. He understands the miracle, and it is no less miraculous for being understood. He calls to her, like he did a decade ago, and she trots, a little unsteadily, to meet him. She crashes into Him like a ballistic missile, knocking Him to the floor so She can lick his face with a silicone tongue.

"Stop it, you!" He says. For just a moment, he is again just a Boy, playing with a rambunctious Dog. But now there is no one telling him to stay away, no Monsters to fight. There is just a Boy and his Dog, and ten years of absence to catch up on.

H.D. Hunter

Natural Life

Ladies and gentlemen of the jury, my client was made strong. Mhm. Made strong by a life of hardships. She has endured levels of tragedy and tribulation untold, catastrophic amounts of personal destruction. She has survived it all.

And now, even this.

Ladies and gentlemen of the jurrreeeey, you have the opportunity to do something tuh-day that has never, *ever* been done. That the State doesn't *want* you to do.

You have the opportunity to make history.

You see, we all understand what a life sentence means, what that entails. We know that in most cases, those sentenced to the rest of their natural lives in prison will die in that very place, or in an infirmary, or in some other small and dismal and wretched stone corner of a colorless fortress. A quarter of all lifers won't ever even get a *sniff* at parole. And the percentage of convicts sentenced to life has increased over **FIF-tee percent** in the last twenny years.

They aren't all monsters, just so you know. No, no. I'm here, ladies and gentlemen of the jury. I'm here ev-er-ry day. This is my job. I see the people the state banishes to a cruel, bedeviled isolation. They are salt and dirt, these people. They are **creek water**, and **mud**, and

red.

Georgia.

clay.

They are real people, ladies and gentlemen. Just like you. Just like me.

Just like my client.

Today, y'all were forced to listen to the prosecution spew speculative theories and ramble on about my client's parentage, her alleged involvement in the occult, her extensive medical history, et cetera, et cetera, and for that I truly apologize, but I must also AD-*vise* that you keep your *eyes* steadfast on the *prize*, ladies and gentlemen.

Of the jury.

Do not be deceived by the misdirection of a team of ... legal tricksters, who, from day one, have done everything in their power to lead you astray.

People are scared of what they can't control. It's natural. I don't blame the prosecution. But me personally, well, I believe some things are meant to exist beyond our understanding. In fact, I have been shown as much by the **scripture** of the **good book,** which says *Trust in the LORD with all thine heart; and lean not unto thine own understanding. In all thy ways acknowledge him, and he shall direct thy paths.*

Now, knowing what we know, I must ask ... who among us could have shown more trust in the Lord than my client? Who could have been so diligent as she, to end up right here, right now? Her presence here is no coincidence, folks. But neither is yours. This is ... of a divine design.

Was not Lazarus – was not *JesusChristhesonofGodhimself* risen out of the darkest of pits for the light to shine upon him once again? So that he might bring blessings to the world and all of God's children? It is simply amazing, ladies and gentlemen of the jury, what a second chance can mean for a person. Was it not

that *very same* Jesus of Nazareth whose own sacrifice paid the cost of a chance at a second and eternal life for

every.
single.
oneofusinthisroomgoodGod-fearingpeopleofWareCounty, Georgia I know you hear me ... I know you feel me in your heart. And it's time for you to make the right decision.

It's time to take your place in history.

My client was sentenced to life in prison, ladies and gentlemen of the jury. She served **thirty years** in a maximum security facility. One of the wickedest, most vile places at which our nation punishes its own imperfect citizens, who seek only redemption.

Last week, ladies and gentlemen, my client died in her cell. Confirmed by the correctional medicine physician on call that night. The prison staff left her there. Shift change, poor record-keeping, faulty communication—call it what you will. But they did not retrieve her body. For thirty-eight hours, they left my client dead in that cell. Cold. Alone. Without dignity.

But in the thirty-ninth hour, ladies and gentlemen of the jury ... my client opened her eyes. With God and a sole 'nother inmate as witness, my client opened her EYES, rose to her FEET, and called out for the correctional officer. And now we're here.

We have no more time today to talk about magic and science. Nay, even the period of bewilderment at God's own miracles has come to its temporary end inside this courtroom. But even if we did, it wouldn't matter. Because the *law* of the State of Georgia says my client's sentence is complete, ladies and

gentlemen. The *law* says her time has been served. There is absolutely **no** valid ground, moral or philosophical, that exists to explain why she should return to incarceration.

They gave her life. She gave her own. And now, she's back.

Good people of Ware County, my client is a free woman.

You know it, I know it, and the prosecution knows it.

It's time to make history.
Make the right decision.

Nia Harris

Ease

And one day you try again once more

The words spill out
The sentences come together

Your hands move effortlessly
Your body flows freely
Your soul speaks

And God is reflected in all that is
All that you are

About the editor

Bri Stokes is a writer, editor, curator, cultural worker, producer, and poet born, raised, and living in Los Angeles, on unceded Tongva land. Her writing has appeared in BuzzFeed, 45th Parallel, Epiphany, the Northridge Review, and elsewhere. Bri is a former poetry editor at the now-disbanded Hecate Magazine and served as the Managing Editor of Issue 04 of SKEW Magazine. Her debut chapbook, A Throat Full of Forest-Dirt, was published in late 2023 by Bottlecap Press. Earlier in 2023, she was longlisted for Thin Air Magazine's "The Bird In Your Hands" prize for poetry. In 2018, she was awarded "Best Short Story" by the El Camino College Myriad for her speculative fiction piece, "Pr(e)y." Bri is a poetry and fiction reader for Epiphany, a 2024 Voodoonauts Fellow, a 2024 Resident with The Seventh Wave Magazine, and an editorial assistant at HINCHAS Press.

About the authors

Shonda Buchanan: Oxfam Ambassador Shonda Buchanan is the author of three collections of poems, including The Lost Songs of Nina Simone, and the award-winning memoir Black Indian, chosen by PBS NewsHour as a "Top 20 books to read to learn about institutional racism." Assistant Professor in the Department of English at Western Michigan University and faculty in Alma College's MFA Program in Creative Writing, Shonda has published in The Mississippi Review, Tab Review, Red Ink Review, the Los Angeles Times, the LA Weekly, Indian Country Today, Capital & Main, Westways Magazine, Sisters of AARP and the Los Angeles Times Magazine. Thrice Pushcart Prize nominee, a Best of the Net nominee, and a California Arts Council Established Artist Fellow, Shonda is a USC Los Angeles Institute for the Humanities Fellow and a City of Los Angeles (COLA) Department of Cultural Affairs Master Artist Fellow. An English Language Specialist with the Department of State and PEN Emerging Voices Fellow and Mentor, Shonda's works-in-progress are America's Bloodflowers and Children of the Mixed Blood Trail. For more information, visit www.shondabuchanan. com.

Kuahmel: Soul Brother No. 7 has crossed many paths, serving as a headline feature artist at events all over California. Alum of Project Blowed, Still Waters Writers' Workshop, Spoken Literature Art Movement, and other collectives. Admissions director with Community Literature initiative, turning over 100 poets into published authors. Quotes on the Lake Superior State University Banished Words List in 2010, 2011, and 2014. Albums ...On The Fly and Call It An Album! Books: Knowledge of Self, Sounds from the Waters, and Peace in the Pocket. Host of many mic series from Project Blowed to Mic Influence. Much more coming from poet, music maker, social commentator, and humorist Kuahmel.

Nia Harris: Nia Harris is a queer Black femme with deep roots in Catawba, Tuscarora, and Lumbee tribal lands (Eastern North Carolina). She lives out her purpose as a community health practitioner, birth worker, land tender, and storyteller through her practice, Healing Us Evergreen (HUE). In her writing, Nia reflects on being of service in community, recounts personal healing experiences, and dreams of liberation for all. Her work is currently published on HUE's website and in Oregon Humanities.

Daniel Pizarro: Daniel Pizarro is a first-generation Peruvian and Puerto Rican non-binary queer living in Atlanta, GA, and a community organizer working at the intersections of abolition, disability, decolonization, and immigration. Pizarro's creative writing explores themes of collective liberation, faith, magic, and justice.

Professionally, Pizarro serves as the Organizing Manager with New Disabled South, advancing disability justice by building political power with and for disabled people in the South. Pizarro also holds an M.A. in Anthropology and a graduate certificate in Women's, Gender, and Sexuality Studies from Georgia State University.

Esteban Silva: Esteban Gaspar Silva is a Mexican immigrant educator, storyteller, and community organizer based in Brooklyn, NY. Through his work as a high school teacher, he explores the intersection of cultural identity and narrative, developing an innovative curriculum that connects literary genres like Magical Realism, Afro-futurism, and Cyberpunk with social justice. His creative practice spans multiple mediums, including music, poetry, and short fiction, examining themes of queerness, immigration, and economic liberation. He also releases music under the name Curanderx://

Lisa Bradley: A queer, disabled Latina originally from South Texas, Lisa M. Bradley now lives in Iowa, the traditional homeland of the Iowa, Ponca, and Winnebago tribes and the Meskwaki Nation, among others. Her work has been featured on the LeVar Burton Reads podcast and in venues such as The Magazine of Fantasy and Science Fiction, Lightspeed, Beneath Ceaseless Skies, and Uncanny. Her short fiction and poetry collection is The Haunted Girl (Aqueduct Press). Her debut novel is Exile (Rosarium Publishing). She is a poetry editor for Strange Horizons and also coedited, with R.B. Lemberg, the Ursula Le Guin tribute poetry anthology, Climbing Lightly Through Forests. Learn more at www.lisambradley.com or follow her on Bluesky, @cafenowhere.bsky.social.

Buhlebethu Mpofu: Buhlebethu Sukoluhle Mpofu is a 31-year-old Zimbabwean writer who enjoys crafting stories that explore the human experience. Through their writing, Mpofu aims to create narratives that resonate with readers and bridge different perspectives. Reading has always been Mpofu's escape and inspiration, leading them to develop their storytelling voice. Mpofu balances a passion for writing with other studies.

Lucy Zhang: Lucy Zhang writes, codes, and watches anime. Her work has appeared in Virginia Quarterly Review, Shenandoah, The Massachusetts Review, and elsewhere. Find her at https://lucyzhang.tech or on Twitter @Dango_Ramen.

Lysz Flo: Lysz Flo is an AfroCaribbean Latine, polyglot, word artist, and indie author, member of The Estuary Collective, Ignyte Awards Winner for CNF, Creatively Exposed podcast host, Voodoonauts Summer 2020 Fellow/Educator in 2024, and Obsidian Black Listening 2022 Fellow. She released her poetry novel, Soliloquy of an Ice Queen, in March 2020. She has been a creative educator since 2020 and has a writing workshop series in MOCA NOMI. Her poems can be found in FIYAH, Hellebore, Lolwe, and Strange Horizons, and she has done various multimedia projects with O' Miami. She is also an Online Crystal and Spiritual wellness shop owner at Astrolyszics.com.

Antoinëtte Van Sluytman: Antoinëtte Van Sluytman is an afrolatinx scholartist and an accomplished artist in a range of media. Her work has been showcased in many prominent art shows in San Diego, and she has won multiple Scholastic Art and Writing awards from the Alliance for Young Writers & Artists for her illustration, poetry, and short fiction. Her debut short fiction was published by Hexagon SF magazine. Antoinëtte is a writer, illustrator, graphic designer, and UCLA Editing & Publishing Extension Instructor on Decolonizing Publishing.

Antoinëtte lectures on the literary circuit about the essence of decolonizing fiction and countering literary imperialism in the industry. Julie Crisp represents Antoinëtte at the Julie Crisp Literary Agency.

Cherokee Collier: Cherokee Rose Collier is a recent graduate of DePaul University, studying Writing and Publishing. With an adoration for the minds of Octavia Butler and Emily Dickinson, Cherokee values stories with a sense of speculation, beauty, and a touch of horror. Cherokee currently resides in Chicago, working on whichever story comes next.

Crystal Davis: Crystal Davis is an Asian-American multidisciplinary and mixed-media performance artist, poet, painter, freelance writer, editor, and social media marketer. Born and raised in Jersey City, New Jersey, she is the author and creator of Crystal Letters, and the Co-Founder and Co-Producer of OpenRoad Poetry, an artistic partnership with RescuePoetix TM.

Her art and writing projects, CL and ORP, have collaborated with arts non-profit organizations and artists across the Tri-State area, nationally, and internationally. Her work is inspired by nature, color, and the utilization of practical craft through art in the visual and written form. Crystal is the author of Elemental Emotions and upcoming books, Softened by Dew and Dark Matter.

Crystal Letters LLC provides freelance editing, writing, poetry, abstract illustrations, mixed media painting, public relations, and social media marketing services. All services are available to artists, poets, collaborators, arts organizations, non-profits, and for-profit organizations from all artistic walks of life. Find her at: www.crystalletters.com.

Lilly Lu: Lilly Lu is a queer Chinese diasporic writer based in Southern California. Lu's short fiction has appeared in venues such as Yuzu Press, Prismatica Magazine, and Heartlines Spec, and my middle-grade debut, SEVEN, will be published in 2026 with Atheneum Books for Young Readers. By day, Lu is an assistant professor of literature at UCSD. By night, Lu is probably watching a show about vampires.

Russell Nichols: Russell Nichols is a speculative fiction writer and endangered journalist. Raised in Richmond, California, he got rid of all his stuff in 2011 to live out of a backpack with his wife, vagabonding around the world ever since. Look for him at russellnichols.com.

Shaira Chaer: Shaira Chaer (b.1989) is a first-generation Dominican-American researcher, writer, and multi-hyphenate creative born and raised on unceded Lenape land in the Bronx, New York. Chaer has written cultural critiques and essays for Remezcla, Vibe Magazine, and more. They have shown work at Bronx Arts Space, Andrew Freedman Home, New Women Space, and Junior High Gallery.

Nick "squidpizza" Cuevas: Squidpizza (meatspace name Nick Cuevas) is a sad, gay author from Texas. Forever chasing impossible dreams, he tells stories nobody else can tell (mostly about sad gay people).

He tells stories because it's the only way to truly communicate his thoughts and feelings. Words are a fundamentally limited medium, as all mediums are, and only through the kaleidoscopic lens of storytelling can truth be gleaned.

He enjoys media analysis and gushing about cute animals, such as horseshoe crabs and leeches.

Sherese Francis: Sherese Francis (she/they) describes themselves as an AlkyMist of the I-Magination, finding expression through poetry, interdisciplinary arts (collage, book and paper arts, sound and performance art, text art), workshop facilitation, editing, and literary curation. Her(e) work takes inspiration from her(e) Afro-Caribbean heritage (Barbados and Dominica), and studies in Afrofuturism and Black Speculative Arts, mythology, and etymology. Some of their work has been published in Furious Flower, Obsidian, Rootwork Journal, The Caribbean Writer, The Operating System, Cosmonauts Avenue, No Dear, Apex Magazine, Bone Bouquet, African Voices, Newtown Literary, and Free Verse. Additionally, Sherese has published four chapbooks, Lucy's Bone Scrolls (Three Legged Elephant, 2017), Variations on Sett/ling Seed/ling (Harlequin Creature, 2018), Recycling a Why That Rules Over My Sacred Sight (DoubleCross Press, 2021) and Lady Liberty Smashing Stones (THRASH Press, 2022), and edited a poetry anthology/guided journal, Baby Suggs and a Purple Butterfly (Get Fresh Books, 2024). Sherese has received grants and awards from Queens Council on the Arts, NYFA, NYSCA, and The Caribbean Writer, residencies from WorksonWater, LMCC, Akademie Schloss Solitude, and SeaSalted Honey in Senegal, and fellowships from Voodoonauts and Baldwin for the Arts.

Tylyn Johnson: Tylyn K. Johnson (they/he) is a floating writer from Naptown, IN. He writes to reflect a complex love through the framed lenses of Black Queer artistry. Their language appears in Lolwe, Toyon Literary Magazine, just femme and dandy, and The Indianapolis Review, among other spaces. He is the creator of "Communal Creativity: A Game of Poetry" on itch.io. Tylyn has also shown work at the Indianapolis Central Library and Circle City Industrial Complex. In 2024, one of their poems was muralized as part of the Indy Arts Council Sidewalk Galleries.

When Tylyn isn't rambling with family and friends, writing, or contemplating their place in the world, they can usually be found fawning over art—local, online, and international.

Linktree (Projects/Social Media): linktr.ee/tykywrites

Molara Wood: Molara Wood is a writer, journalist, and editor based in Lagos, Nigeria. She is the author of Indigo, a collection of short stories. She won the John La Rose Memorial Short Story Competition and received an award from the British Broadcasting Association for her fiction.

H.D. Hunter: Hugh "H.D." Hunter is a storyteller, teaching artist, and community organizer from Atlanta, Georgia. He's the author of Torment: A Novella and Something Like Right, as well as the winner of several international indie book awards for multicultural fiction. You can find his work online in Porter House Review.

Hugh is also the author of the Futureland series, including Battle for the Park, which was named a Georgia Center for the Book 2023 Book All Young Georgians Should Read, and the 2023-2024 VAReads Chapter Book of the Year. Battle for the Park is also a 2024 selection for the CORE Excellence in Children's Science Fiction Notable list. Futureland: The Nightmare Hour and Futureland: The Architect Games are the second and third books in the series.

Hugh is an alum of the inaugural Tin House Young Adult Fiction Workshop. He's served as both a moderator and panelist at FIYAHCON. He's a "cocoa" founder of the Voodoonauts Summer Fellowship for Black speculative fiction writers, and his teaching credits include PocketMFA, Clarion West Online, Catapult, and a Writer-in-Residence position with the PEN/Faulkner Foundation.

Hugh is committed to stories about Black kids and their many expansive worlds. Connect with Hugh on Instagram (@hdhunterbooks) or his website: hughhdhunter.com.

Trinity Lee: Trinity Lee is an African-American girl from Chicago who currently lives in sunny Arizona. Because of her culture and gender, Lee has always been acutely aware of difference. Growing up, there weren't many spaces where she could fit in, but she felt most confident, capable, and beautiful whenever she would write. Lee has described herself as having "a healthy amount of angst," and put it all towards a BA in women and gender studies, volunteering, crafting, and working at a non-profit cafe that helps her community.

Kelsey L. Smoot: Kelsey L. Smoot (They/Them/He/Him) is a full-time PhD student in the interdisciplinary social sciences and humanities. They are also a poet, advocate, and frequent writer of critical analysis. Kelsey is the winner of the 2021 Sad Girls Girl's Club Literary Contest, the 2023 The Good Life Review Honeybee Prize, and the Grand Prize Winner of the 2024 Button Poetry Video Contest. He is a Pushcart Prize nominee, a Best of the Net nominee, as well as the author of a chapbook titled we was bois together with CLASH! (An Imprint of Mouthfeel Press).

Najah Hylton: Najah Amatullah Hylton, Master of Arts in literature, is a lifelong writer and performer. She taught secondary English language arts for eleven years. She has devoted her energy to enhanced secondary curriculum, blogs, video podcasts, poetry, and public speaking. She is the co-author of the children's book Opal's Greenwood Oasis, the poet behind Jabee's hip hop album Black Future, and co-creator of a book of curriculum for the hip-hop album Fire in Little Africa. Najah has two self-published books of poetry: The Risk to Bloom from 2014 and Dangerously Absurd Places from 2023.

HINCHAS Press

About us

HINCHAS Press is a Los Angeles-based micropress that publishes zines, poetry, poetry in translation, and library science non-fiction. HINCHAS supports social justice initiatives, and advocates for bilingual literacy endeavors, especially along portions of the Américas that are monolingual.

HINCHAS Press seeks to showcase the fiction, poetry, and prose of authors from las América and America. In terms of taste and content, we firmly believe the content to be the medium. To that end, we seek to publish innovative, experimental work of a devastating caliber, regardless of format, dialect, or pedigree.

HINCHAS
Press

www.ingramcontent.com/pod-product-compliance
Lightning Source LLC
Chambersburg PA
CBHW040534170726
48295CB00012B/459